MEHER BABA'S WORD
AND HIS THREE
BRIDGES

MEHER BABA'S
WORD
AND HIS THREE
BRIDGES

DON E. STEVENS

WITH NORAH MOORE *&* LAURENT WEICHBERGER

Companion Books
PUBLISHERS

Published by
Companion Books
London

Second Edition, April 19, 2021.

FRONT COVER PHOTO
Avatar Meher Baba at Upper Meherabad,
India July 30, 1941
©2021 by MSI Collection (Christine & Martin Cook).
Photographed by Padri. Used by permission.

BACK COVER PHOTO
Don Stevens visits Khuldabad,
Sufi Valley of the Saints, Arangabad Marahashtra,
India during 2005.
Photo by Martin Cook.

*Meher Baba stands on the line of demarcation
between God, the Light, & his Creation, the shadow.*

*Notice how the whole photo revolves around
the central figure of Baba, and yet he blends
almost totally into the background.*

*His chest and heart merge with the Light
that pours in through the window,
as there is no actual boundary
between God and Baba.*

❖

Table of Contents

Song of the New Life

Listen to the silent words of Meher Baba;
The life of all lovers of God is in these words.
You who are serious to follow the New Life
Will renounce your ephemeral existence.

We have taken to this life in which we rely only upon God;
Our will is strengthened by our oath.
We merrily sing the song of hopelessness;
We invite all calamities and difficulties.

We neither wail over lost hopes, nor complain about promises,
Or covet honor, or shun disgrace.
Back-biting is ended and we do not fear anyone;
This is the tenor of our New Life.

No confusion in the mind now, neither are any ties left;
Pride, anger, lust and greed are sloughed off.
No religion for any of us, nor care for physical and mental aims.
The Sheikh and the Brahmin are now in the same boat.

There is for us all no small or great.
Neither disciple, master, nor Godhood exist.
Brotherliness is the link,
And our common enjoyment of suffering.

This world or the next, hell or heaven, we are no longer concerned with.
Shaktis and siddhis, occultism and miracles, we are no longer plagued with.
All false impressions have been purged from the mind;
Now we live with the active present.

Dear ones, take seriously the words of Baba.
"Although now I am on the same level with you,
Yet all orders from me, good, bad, or extraordinary,
You should carry out immediately, leaving the result to God.

"Even if the heavens fall,
Do not let go the hand of Truth;
Let despair and disappointment ravage and destroy the garden of your life;
You beautify it by contentment and self-sufficiency.

"Even though your heart be cut to bits, let a smile be on your lips.
Here I divulge to you a truth:
Hidden in your empty hands is treasure untold;
Your beggarly life is the envy of kings.

"God exists indeed, and true are the Prophets,
Every cycle has an Avatar, and every moment a wali.
For us, however, it is only hopelessness and helplessness,
How else can I describe to you what our New Life is?"

Source : *Tales from the New Life with Meher Baba*,
Narrated by Eruch, Mehera, Mani and Meheru,
©1976 by Avatar Meher Baba Perpetual Public Charitable Trust
[corrected]

Introduction to the Second Edition

DON STEVENS WAS CONCERNED that people have methods to directly and individually access Meher Baba's guidance. He served as a tireless editor to Meher Baba's works, God Speaks, as well as Listen, Humanity, and the Discourses. In addition to reading Meher Baba's words, he saw group work as an important method for people to learn from each other and to be able to develop their own personal tools to communicate directly with Meher Baba. Meetings with Don were not lectures, but were forums for exchange and a flow of Baba conversation. The delight of this book is that it captures some of that special ambience and spirit that animated group meetings with Don. This approach aligned with the sort of give and take exchanges that would take place with the Baba lovers and resident mandali at Meherazad, in Mandali Hall. Don would also draw on his direct experience of his personal meetings with Meher Baba in Mandali Hall, even to the extent that when the "Parvardigar Prayer" would be said at one of his meetings, Don would insist that it be read aloud by just one person, which is the way that it had been done in Baba's presence at Meherazad.

Meher Baba was a great communicator, and Baba would often remind Don that, as He too lived in the world, Baba willingly became limited by the constraints associated with having a gross body. This was first forcefully pointed out to Don by Baba on the occasion of Don's mother's death. Thinking Baba just knew such things, Don had neglected to tell Baba that his mother had passed away. When the fact of her death came to Baba's attention through conversation with Baba, Baba instructed Don that he needed to communicate with Baba by the "most handy physical means possible." In a follow up to that instruction, Baba had asked Don to report to him anything that happened to him of "great or of medium importance." Over time, Don tells us that simply using his physical voice to converse with Baba seemed to effectively carry out that instruction. One caveat that Don would often bring up is that he believed that his regular reporting to Baba should not be for the purpose of asking anything of Baba, but rather to simply inform Him of what was going on in his life.

Whether Baba was gesturing a communication, using a facial expression, hugging a devotee, holding their hand, kissing them on the cheek (or side of the neck), or meticulously spelling out a word, he put a tremendous effort into communicating with human beings. In Don's experience, Baba would at times take great care in his method of giving and reviewing certain messages to which he gave special importance. It was in reference to such messages that Meher Baba explained to Don that Baba had attached something on the order of an atom bomb of spiritual energy to these words, which would give enormous and unfolding help to the spiritual aspirant in their ongoing journey.

As with much of Don's work, this book is the outcome of a team effort of its participants and coordinators, to allow space for a wonderfully productive and lively atmosphere to arise. Both Laurent Weichberger and Norah Moore had been appointed on this occasion to serve as Don's "wing-people," and help Don navigate the delivery and exploration of the enormous amount of information that Don wished to see covered in a weekend conversion in his London home at Hammersmith Grove.

Richard and Cynthia Griffin
Salem, Massachusetts
JUNE 7, 2021

Prelude

I AM SITTING ON A TRAIN going down from London, where I was working all week with Don at his apartment, back to my West Sussex home. This has rapidly become a routine. Ironically, the stop where I always get off is called "Three Bridges," as that is the closest station to where I live. Today was a landmark day, as I finished transcribing the recordings of Don's seminar: *Meher Baba's Word and His Three Bridges* which was presented in May 2003. This entire book is based on the complete transcript of what we all shared that wonderful weekend.

Half of the transcripts have been prepared by Jenny and Craig Zenner, and Ann McEvoy in Myrtle Beach. I was responsible for providing the other half, and have been transcribing on and off since May, between teaching Java, work and travel with Don, and spending time with my (very patient) family. Don himself completed almost all of the preliminary editing of this book in a huge push during June 2003, when he sat for more than a week (sometimes eight or more hours a day) at Ed Legum's home office near Atlanta, Georgia. Don painstakingly reviewed, word by word, all that he shared over the two seminar days to be sure that it was as accurate as possible for publication. I am doing a second pass over it all now, and then we will fire it off to Ed for the layout and graphic design work, which he has obviously mastered.

As soon as I would finish a section of transcript, no matter where I was in the world, I would find out where Don was and get it to him immediately. Don and I spent this most-last week together at his London flat, me with my lap-top at the dining room table, and Don in his bedroom office (at his computer) finalizing this process until today, when we are just about done. It feels so right.

The funny thing is that I only just met Don a little over a year ago, during one of his *God Speaks* seminars, at the Meher Spiritual Center in Myrtle Beach. At that time I had no intention of living in England, let alone sitting next to Don for a day while he presented about the last fifty years of his life working with and for Meher Baba. I am still a little disoriented, to say the least.

You should know that Don roped me into writing this prelude. He has a way with people. I will take this opportunity to share a little bit about who Don Stevens is, for those who may not know, and even take a few risks. Hey, you only live eight million four hundred thousand times, right? I feel authorized to share, not just because I have been asked by him to do so, but because I moved to England for the purpose of writing Don's biography, with a small team of Baba-followers. I have spent the last year studying this man, his life and work, his relationships, and more importantly his relationship with Meher Baba. Don is one of the few people about whom I can wholeheartedly say everything about his life is a dedication to Baba as the "Living Master." It is amazing to see Don in action. At age eighty-four, he keeps a pace and schedule that would wear out at twenty-four year old. He is in perpetual motion, unless he is asleep. He tends to friends and nurtures relationships all over the world. He always has a number of projects in various states of progress (also all over the world), and all revolving around the central theme of his life, Avatar Meher Baba.

This reminds me of an interview I did with one of Don's close friends, Lady Wedgwood, who lives near here in Lewes. I asked about her impression of Don, and she was happy to share. First she quoted her teacher, Vilayat Khan, the son of Hazrat Inayat Khan, "You don't argue about God, you meet Him." Then she continued with her own understanding, "That is the difference between a mystic and a theologian. With a *theologian*, it is about argument. With a *mystic*, it is about love. Then she quoted Evelyn Underhill, "You know your true Mystic because they are very practical people." And then she wrapped it all up, in her own unique style and wit, *"When you think of Don, sitting at his computer, writing books in different languages, at a moments notice, that's practical."* It is so true. Don is such a wild mix of practical, creative, mystical, loving, intellectual, and much more. I know he has a reputation for being too-intellectual, but anyone who says that has not felt his tremendous warmth of feeling, his true sensitivity and love for all things human and natural.

Don proceeds with child-like simplicity at times, and then can suddenly switch into high powered business mode, based on decades of a career as Research Chemist and then Vice President at Chevron Oil company. Meher Baba has said so many things directly about Don that I couldn't possibly attempt to weigh down these few pages with them. Suffice it to say, Baba declared in more ways than one, "Don Stevens is My Man," and revealed on multiple occasions that Don was one of his Mandali. For more, read his biography, *An Almost Perfect Balance* (you won't be disappointed).

This small volume, *Meher Baba's Word and His Three Bridges*, is the clear reflection of Baba's Man Don, and it is jam packed with deep sharing, emotionally charged issues, priceless stories, fantastic ideas, contemplative questions, and much more. Don't let its size fool you. I predict it will go down in history as one of the most important books in the Meher Baba literature. What is more amazing to me is that unlike many of the gatherings I have attended in the Baba community, over more than fifteen years, Don makes it a point to invite everyone's vision, everyone's experience. He repeatedly opens the floor for all to participate and interact (even when it is not comfortable to do so). In fact, this is one of the hallmarks of what Don appears to be pushing as an agenda for the New Humanity.

If I could put my understanding of Don's seminar method into words, it would be something like, "The time has come to do away with the old patterns of students sitting with hands folded, facing the front of the room listening to the teacher, guru, guide, Murshid, Master, or Mandali, (or whatever) and begin to trust one another, open our hearts to one another, expose our minds to one another, share deeply about what the life of the spirit means to each one of us in light of our dedication to our Beloved Avatar, Meher Baba. And in this process, to intentionally link with one another, in a small circle, in order to move closer to the Beloved in All." Even more radical is that he bases all of his conclusions on the life, work and words of Meher Baba himself. It is truly astounding.

It is all so simple, but appears quite extreme to many. There are so many intense themes running through Don's ongoing work for Baba that it is exceedingly challenging to squeeze them briefly in here, but a few stand out more clearly in contrast to the rest. No doubt the concept of "balancing the head and the heart" will be looked upon as pivotal to the progress of the spiritual seeker, even if it is initially met with resistance. Even in these last three months I have found that I am more aware of the importance of this issue, more mindful of when my head is taking over, and when my heart is being pushed out of the ring. More sensitive to how this affects others.

Many of the issues raised during the seminar are so intricate and huge that it is abundantly clear we only managed to scratch the surface. Some of them are potentially explosive, but at least the issues are no longer being hidden, and labeled unspeakable. We could go on for two weeks, two months, even two years or more with many of the topics Don had typed up for his two-day presentation outline. It was an ambitious agenda, and he did his best. Another theme that was brought to light is the extraordinarily hot potato, the "Judas factor" which will doubtless be debated, at least in Baba circles, for the next two centuries at least. This issue had previously been labeled "untouchable in public," and yet Don is so passionate these days it is truly inspiring. This was the biggest risk of all, and I am proud of him (if I can say that) for going way out on that limb.

Don seems uninterested, even fed-up (I know I am) with the old format for a Baba gathering or Sahavas. He wants to see real sharing, real connecting, even deep linking between companions on the path, not teaching or just telling the same stories, over & over. I tell him he is a late bloomer, because it seems to me that this, right now, is the best of Don Stevens. It is as if he is only now harvesting the fruits of five decades in Baba's service, & moreover he is eager to share these fruits with all.

On a final note, for what it is worth, the seminar format is a tough one, where many forces are flowing, and the current of the conversation is fast and deep. Not everyone present spoke at the seminar, but even the presence of those who remained silent was greatly valued. Also, some that did speak were not able to fully express their viewpoint. When so many people gather and try to discuss such profound subjects, invariably someone has to just let it go, and pick up the thread of discussion later. I saw this happen repeatedly to us all.

Another fascinating part of the process of creating a book from a seminar is realizing the tremendous difference between how the seminar sounds, as compared to the printed version. It is impossible to communicate in typed format the tones, timbre, implications, connotations, resonance, and subtleties that are conveyed clearly with sound. Initially I found this to be a serious block. I feared the transcripts would fail to accurately convey what transpired at the seminar, and maybe even confuse people. For this reason we have worked inordinately hard to edit this book carefully so that many different aspects of what transpired at the seminar are faithfully transmitted, and the meaning is as clear as possible. I hope the reader will sense on the breeze a real fragrance of what emerged. For my part, I am just a fledgling falcon watching a great golden eagle soar towards the One, the Divine Beloved Avatar Meher Baba.

Uh-oh, next stop, *Three Bridges*.

LAURENT WEICHBERGER, July 10, 2003

MEHER BABA'S WORD
AND HIS THREE
BRIDGES

Live Seminar
Presented by Don Stevens
at the Meher Baba Association
London, England

Saturday, May 3, 2003 &
Sunday, May 4, 2003

10:00 AM to 12:00 PM &
2:00 PM to 4:00 PM
both days

1 : Saturday Morning

DON: ONE THING I WOULD LIKE TO DO is make two introductions. I think most of you have met one way or another by now, but some of you perhaps still not, my two pillars (my leaning posts) for the two days, because I always have to have someone to prop me up in case I fall over, you see. So, Dr. Norah Moore, who has been in the Sunday study group for what, almost two years now, isn't it, Norah?

Norah: Yes.

⁋ Don: Yes, it makes her tired just to think about it. {laughter from audience} A lot of work goes on there. I'll tell you just a little bit about her background. Norah, I think, first heard of Baba from Craig San Roque, & almost everyone here has been around Craig at some point or another. So, Craig studied under Norah in the Jungian Institute, as Norah is a pillar in the Jungian Institute, and she is also a practicing psychoanalyst. She doesn't practice it on us incidentally … or if she does, she is very quiet about it.

Norah: I can't even think about it!

⁋ Don: Well, anyway, she is a lovely person and a lovely pillar, and a good buttress. So, she'll be getting a few questions tossed at her by Don (you know my bad habit) during the day, but she always rises. Then tomorrow, another pillar, who has been mostly an e-mail correspondent, even though for a relatively short of time. He's sitting here with his sweet gal Aspen, who's now starting school down in Sussex, and I think has already had a week, haven't you Aspen?

Aspen: Mmm.

⁋ Don: Mmm?

Aspen: Yeah.

¶ Don: About a week, um-hm, yeah. And I even hear rumors it's going awfully well so that's a ... well, she looks just a little bit ... her eyes are turning, you can't see them, but I think that's not quite all the story. At any rate, the second pillar is Laurent Weichberger. We ran into each other he says, donkey's years ago, in Meher Baba House in New York City ...

Laurent: Yeah.

¶ Don: I think he must have been, you know, one of those strapping ... No, you weren't strapping. I think you were very thin in those days, a very skinny teenager probably, and I don't remember Laurent at all in any case. But all of a sudden he pops up in my e-mail and said [something like] – Don, I know that you were one of the perpetrators of *God in A Pill?* You remember, the quotations that Baba sent to the three people that he sent out from the Boston universities, who did a helluva good job. And so, eventually Baba sent back word that he thought it would be a good idea if Murshida Duce (or whomever she would like to pick) would select from his various instructions to them various things that he had said about drugs. Murshida Duce had a way, at that particular time of life, of saying, "Well, Don, you're handy with words, so why don't you take on this job?" So I stuck together (pasted together) *God in A Pill?* and had really a terrifically good time doing it.

At any rate, rather recently the job fell to Laurent to update and revise anything necessary in *God in A Pill?* and as he was finishing it off he thought – Well, maybe that old so-and-so Stevens ought to be brought into the act here before we close up shop and go to the printer – so he got in touch with me via e-mail. Now I have to tell you one characteristic that struck me right away after I had exchanged two e-mails with Laurent. I said to myself – This guy is a shaker and a doer.

If you're not American, you may not know what that means, but he shakes things up and gets things done. That's putting it in a nutshell. So, we gradually got to know each other, actually, in person, almost a year now, and Laurent and family have moved to the South of England, and he probably is starting to think already, this is getting too close to the scene of the crime! At any rate he's still shaking things up and doing things, so he will be the pillar for tomorrow. Now, enough introductions, but they are two awfully good people, so get them off in a corner and get to know them.

Now I want to tell you that there are really two principal reasons for my deciding after a couple of really strenuous years with *God Speaks* seminars, why I did this absolutely insane thing [of starting a new series of seminars] in my old age. Suddenly, something about the long history of Baba's writings, and some of the things that Baba had told me as this or that assignment would get assigned, and that one would start, and so on, there were two things that finally brought this to a head. First of all was the fiftieth anniversary of Baba's accident in Oklahoma.

Now by any chance has anyone here been to where that accident occurred? You were there, Laurent? Were you there at the time that the fiftieth anniversary was going on?

Laurent: No, but I wanted to be.

Don: Yes, but you drove through, did you?

Laurent: Well, I made a special point of going there, yes.

Don: Well, it was fifty years ago, not so many weeks ago now, when we got that absolutely horrifying news that Baba and the Mandali had been in an accident in Oklahoma, and Baba and two or three of the women Mandali were badly injured in the process. It was unbelievable! I just can't tell you how shook up we all felt. It's the sort of thing that you know inside of you can't happen, and there it did happen. So, they had a really tremendous [fiftieth anniversary] remembrance. The Love Street Lamp Post published a good big long summary, and it was really very beautifully done. Dina Snow does marvelous work on the Lamp Post, as Maxine [Summers] has done on the Newsletter, and as Richard Turner is doing now.

So there it was, the great big long history of it, and they actually decided to set up a little memorial, on the spot. I believe that the money has been collected and that it is a done thing already. But as I was reading all of this, and noting that it was the fiftieth anniversary, that really shook me up because it just seemed to me like it was yesterday, Marion, and here it is fifty years ago. {Marion Saunders is sitting in the front row} And of course that was on Baba's first visit to America after the 30s.

[The accident] was a tremendously important occasion. We on the West Coast were looking forward to Baba's imminent arrival, of course, and then, to have this happen. So it was doubly earth shaking for all of us. [The fiftieth anniversary memorial of his accident] reminded me of the fact that it also had to be fifty years ago that I first met Baba face to face, which is quite a memorial for me, too. But also, what really startled me was that I realized – *My God, I've been working on Baba's words and his assignments to me for fifty years now,* Can you imagine? Because that's when he warned Murhsida Duce and me that he was very busy writing something or another, and that if we would take on the editing of the manuscript, he would send it over just as soon as possible. And of course, that was *God Speaks*. So [this was the occasion when] *God Speaks* first got mentioned by Baba. I don't think he gave the title at that point, I think it was only when it came over to us and I opened up the manuscript that I saw this: "God Speaks", —Oh my God. Well, there we are, more about that later on.

At any rate, that's fifty years ago. And since they were having

a fiftieth anniversary about Baba's accident, that made me think
– Well, fifty long years, this is sort of special for me, too. I ought
to do something obvious. So this was the very, very, very first
thing that made me decide that I should do something fairly important, because that's quite a heritage. And of course, an awful
lot of those years from 1952 until 1969 were spent constantly and
vigorously on the projects under Baba's thumb.

When this ball of fire Balaji (I'm really anxious to get Laurent
and Balaji together, because when two balls of fire meet you never know what sort of a cataclysm is going to get let loose), but
it was just last year when Balaji arranged a couple of big public
meetings (three or four, maybe it was even five). He said, "Don
this is going to be a nice easy trip, nothing exciting happening
… " So we had some of the biggest congregations of Baba-lovers
I've ever been around, all expecting words of wisdom, of course.

I told them in general some of the story of some of the [book
project] things, how they came about, what Baba expected and
some of the time limits Baba put upon them. I think it was six
weeks we had to do the major editing on *God Speaks*. Does that
shock you? *Well it sure shocked the hell out of us.* {laughter}

I told them the story that when the manuscript actually arrived in New York (Lud Dimpfl brought it over from India, he
had just been there to see Baba), he passed it on to Murshida in
New York, and she had been quickly running over it (we will
get more into the details of all of that). I was on a business trip
in the Eastern United States for Standard Oil of California, and
I had had my next two-three months plotted out in great detail
by my President.

Now here you have a book called *God Speaks* laid on your
knees, and six weeks to get it edited and you're in the middle of
a field trip and, you know, rustling around on this train and that
airplane and staying in this crazy hotel and out with sometimes

crazier people (all with problems of course) isn't this the ideal environment to work on *God Speaks*? {more laughter}

So back to Balaji's meetings last year. I was telling them about this, and you should have seen the looks on those Indian people. They just couldn't believe it, you know, something like that ... how would our dear Beloved Baba ever allow? ... That was bad planning!

But they didn't dare mention it, even in their minds ... you can't criticize Baba, you love him too much. So here I was, and when I saw the look on these Indian people, you know, they've never forgotten it. I get this story fed back to me by almost everybody ... Somebody who was in the audience at this city sent it to somebody else, and they said, "Don this was absolutely incredible, did it really happen that way?"

And do you know, I can't do any sort of creative writing unless I'm in an airplane waiting room, or in a strange hotel or something like that now ... {laughter} That's where I do my best ... {more laughter} Norah, does this make any sense to you?

Norah: Absolutely.

Don: She's a good psychologist, so she can figure these things out.

At any rate, when I saw the looks on these people's faces and saw what an incredible event they had shared, I could see that I had added to their stock of Baba lore & very important happenings.

To return to our base of Baba's word and an important part of how he gave it to us, it being the fiftieth anniversary, I saw clearly that I should certainly get things moving from my side. Many of the things I am going to be saying (especially this morning, and perhaps part of this afternoon) are repetitions of stories that I've trotted out here and there for various reasons, but I just have to ask you please sit through them. I love them all so much. I love re-telling them, and I hope you love re-listening to them because for me they are *real life with Baba*, really wonderful experiences.

There is however another major, major reason that impelled me to offer these recountings, and I'll tell you the story for that one as we open up tomorrow and lay it out in front of you. That is probably, let's say, the guts of some of the most important things that we all have as our responsibility. If you happened to have taken a look at the agenda sheets out there [in the hall entry] you may have noted that I added in, "Meher Baba's Word and His Three Bridges, *and the Fourth-R, Responsibility*." That means responsibility, somewhere, involved with Baba's words. And this is a huge, huge task, and a terribly important thing, and I can't underline it enough. But I do have to tell you about how this Fourth-R Responsibility came about, and the background. I don't see him around today, but Keith Ashton is in the Sunday study group and he has gradually been evolving what he calls the Three-Rs and I think they are very, very exciting.

One of them he says he just sort of learned. I'm sure he won't mind my telling you this story because he's told it to a lot of people, including most of the Sunday people. He says, "I've learned gradually that in a tough situation (or a complex situation) Keith, don't react." That's the first R. He doesn't say there is a D in front of the R, but Reaction is a "baddy." So don't react. And Keith also said the second thing he's gradually found is, "take a bit of time, some way or another, and put a fence up around your life for a few moments and Reflect." So that's the second R.

And I wish Keith was here, because I can never remember his third R. Do you remember it, Lol?

Lol Benbow: Respond.

¶ Don: Respond. Yes, Respond.

Participant: Respond. What was the second one?

¶ Don: Reflect. Quiet time. This is what John Horder and I call the neutral plateau, get it out there real fast. Should we tell them about that tomorrow John?

John: Yes, that would be great!

Don: {To John} We've been around that one together for quite a long time, haven't we? Well, so then, respond. When we were getting this series of seminars plotted up and the material worked out that would get discussed, Keith said to me, "I think really what the seminars are all about is to point out to people, Baba-lovers and devotees, that they have a tremendous responsibility in preserving 'Baba's Word' properly."

There's a bit of a further story on the Fourth-R. Davy, I guess you and I are the only ones who remember the original three Rs: readin', ritin', 'rithmatic. And that shows just about how well educated the [American] pioneers were who started sending their kids to school and they said, "Now you got to learn Readin, Ritin, Ritmatic" all starting with "R" of course.

So now let's go back to the beginning of that visit with Baba in August of 1952. This is certainly the most important pillar in my life. The most important thing to me, of course, is the first time I saw Baba face to face. That's what set up life from that point on. And it also set up all of the basic pillars for the subsequent things that Baba asked me to do in relation to his various writings, his words. I will just tell it to you as it happened.

Do you remember after that terrible accident in Oklahoma, they carried them in a couple of ambulances back to Myrtle Beach, and there they stayed for some weeks. April, May, June passed convalescing, and eventually the word came that in August Baba would be leaving Myrtle Beach and going up to New York to stay there a few days. Then, if people who were planning originally to see him on the West Coast would come to New York, he would set up a time to see them there. Of course, that was absolute top priority for everybody, and we got busy. I have to explain to you just a little bit about the sort of arrangement that I had with my boss, because this was an important part of my life, too, and I want to tell you about it clearly.

From the time that I was employed by Standard Oil of California in their research laboratories, I felt that some way or another I had to straight-level with my boss on exactly what my personal life was, and the top priority in my life was someone called Meher Baba. To do this I had to explain just a little bit that not long after I graduated from the University, things began to happen that I couldn't explain, and I had to use Stewart Edward White's principle that, "If you can't explain something, just put it on file and then perhaps later the explanation might come up." Well my file of "putting it on file" had been getting thicker, and thicker, and thicker and eventually I did some absolutely zany experiments with thought-concentration and gosh that poured the kerosene right on the fire.

I try not to talk too much about them, but that was my great experience with, well, psychic forces. That rather rapidly became a taboo in my life, because of an unfortunate thing that happened, through psychic experiences, to Murshida Martin which really broke her heart and broke mine when she told me about it. This psychic happening put a great big barrier around dabbling with psychic experiments and making too much of psychic experiences.

At any rate, I would tell just a little bit of this to my new boss in Standard Oil and then I would say that this had led me on to a consistent studying of various major schools of esoteric thinking, and the people I had found as my teachers were pretty good ones. And then I found the Sufis, who made great sense to me. I found they accepted such things as psychology and science and a few of those very delicate avenues and fields we have to tread and pass along. Then I went on to explain how this Eastern friend (I

referred to him as a mystic, a philosopher, and so on) had become the head of the Sufis and had enormously impressed me
through his writings. When I arrived at that point in my abbre-
viated story I would then tell him that this was my top priority
in life, and if something should come along that conflicted with
a business engagement, or something that I had been requested
to carry out, I would like to come to him and explain the situation, and ask if I could still observe this top priority in my life.

I remember the first time that happened, when I was in Chevron research (California Research Corporation it was called). To
my utter astonishment, my Boss, who was a good, run of the
mill, highly qualified, very fine research man himself, nodded
his head at me and said, "Don, I am very happy that you explained that to me. I understand it and I can promise you that,
unless something terribly, terribly, important and unexpected is
at stake, I will respect your priority."

That was my first experience of finding out when you are
in an important personal situation, even touching upon so-
called such things as religion (maybe it wasn't religion but I
didn't try to straighten that out in his mind in this first conversation, you know, I was a little discrete about it) that
people in these great big grasping greedy businesses, could
be human beings. And here I was finding this out in one of
what they called the "seven-big-ugly-sisters" of international petroleum, who were supposed to be the greediest and the
worst and the most stampeding of all in running over human
rights. That was my first such experience and it surprised me.

So, I came to him and said, "Meher Baba, whom I told you
about, has gotten over an accident that he had and is coming to
New York and said that on the weekend (Saturday and Sunday),
if I can get there, I will get a chance to meet him. I don't want to
ask for much, but can I leave early Friday afternoon and catch
the overnight plane to New York, and I would like to leave if

necessary even Monday morning and maybe get [back] in the afternoon to the research laboratory."

He replied, "No trouble at all, Don, and I wish you good luck, and it will be an exciting experience." And little did he know … {laughter} It certainly was. So there we are. Golly, it makes me so happy to think back to what a lovely person … John what do you have?

John: Was this 1952?

Don: This was 1952, yes. Murshida Martin had put her order under him just shortly after the end of World War II in '45. And so it was seven years from the time that we got the news that we had a new Boss-man, Spiritual Boss-man, until I actually saw him face to face. But I needed it! I had some real toughies to get worked out inside of myself before I met the Boss-man.

So here we were. I caught the plane, got into New York City early on the Saturday morning and my psychoanalyst friend, Bob Porter, said, "Don, you can use my apartment any way that you want …" and he said, "do you want some breakfast?" I couldn't even think of breakfast, I had had a couple of bites on the plane and my stomach had revolted anyway, and I hadn't slept much, and I am person of very firm physical habits. I am used to digesting at certain times, and going to the toilet at certain times and sleeping at certain times, and when I found out that Baba was the same way, it did my heart good. I could always say, "Yes Baba, I did that … I tried to do that … well I know that's important," you see? We were on the same wavelength already.

So here we are, getting into New York, and I couldn't eat, I couldn't digest, I couldn't go to the toilet, all I could do was try to shave, and I made a mess of that with my electric razor. I think my hand was prematurely going like that {Don shakes his right hand in the air}. You know, a long plane ride with no sleep does strange things to your nerves.

{To Laurent} You can say that again, can't you?

Laurent: Yes.

¶ Don: At any rate, Bob wishes me well, and I take the metro (or the bus, or something) down Central Park, and down the south side of it, and then up a little ways to where Murshida Duce's apartment was on 67th Street, which I knew well.

I go up in the elevator, and I ring on the doorbell, and eventually her daughter Charmian (who was in her – gosh, I guess she was in her mid-teens actually at that time) I knew Charmy from the time that she was quite a young girl. And as you know she just recently passed on. So Charmy was there, and said, "Oh, Don, you made it!"

And I wanted to say, "Just barely!" Or something growly like that, you know, and so she smiled, and I don't know what I said then. She said, "Well, Don, Baba isn't quite ready to see you yet, so you can go upstairs and sit in my room until he is ready." That was great because I felt that I needed a little bit of collecting my thoughts if I could.

Charmy takes me up the steps and opens the door into her room, and – My God, there are two young gals, whom I knew modestly well, gabbling in the window. So this was the environment in which I was going to have to collect my thoughts. I thought to myself – *Oh, my gosh, I don't want to have to say anything to them. If I have to exchange five sentences I won't be ready for Baba. I will be revolted.*

I can see Norith says, "This really makes sense to me." So, you're a good psychologist too, Norith.

There I was, and the two girls looked at me, and I thought – Well, it's going to begin – and I nodded my head. I don't even think I said good morning to them, just sort of nodded my head, and they looked at me and nodded their heads back. And they didn't even say, "Nice to see you, Don," or anything like that. They just went back to exchanging their thoughts. They were gassing away on a window bench looking out over the street. I thought to myself – *Well thank God for that* – and sat down on the edge of Charmian's bed. I was just sitting there and wondering what I should say to Meher Baba. It should be something important, or heartfelt, or esoteric, or deep, or I don't know what, but I ought be able to say something to him. As I was trying to think – What should I say to Meher Baba when I am there with him?, This was a big crisis, Norah. I didn't know what under the sun to do. {Norah Moore is sitting next to Don all day Saturday}

What would you have done, Norah? If it was your first time to stand right in front of Baba, would you say, "Hello, Baba, how are you?"

Norah: I wouldn't have said anything.

Don: You wouldn't have said anything! Well, boy, you certainly stole that one from me. Anyway, as I was sitting there, all of a sudden I felt a funny, funny feeling in my throat. – Oh, oh, I probably caught an edge of a cold on the airplane and I am getting a sore throat and I hope it's not a bad one, I thought. Then it gave a terrific jab, and I thought – Oh, oh, it's going to be a bad one – and then all of a sudden you know what happened? It afflicted my eyes. I thought – My God, it's gone up into my eyes already – and then tears started. I had never had a cold like this one. Then all of a sudden it struck me: My God. I'm crying. Isn't that absolutely incredible? The last time I had cried was when my collie dog died when I was sixteen years old and he was fifteen, and now I was in my early thirties, and it's been a long time since I cried. And the thing that absolutely flabbergasted me was I didn't know what I was crying about. I wasn't sad. I was out of sorts, my digestion wasn't right, but I never cry about things like that.

So here I am, faced with this, and two girls sitting over there. And I was afraid one of them would look at me and see old staid stable Stevens, with tears rolling down his cheeks, and what if this got out public, you know? Permanently ruin-dicated [that is Stevens slang, it means horribly ruined] ... So I look at them, and try to sniff-sniff and get it down quietly, you know, so they wouldn't know what was going on.

{Don to back row of audience} Can you all hear me over there? This is carrying all right? Sometimes when I get thoughtful like this my voice goes a little further down, so wave your hand, Wayne, if it goes too far.

There I am, and finally I get it under control and [the girls] have been so busy gabbling with each other that neither one of them has seen this incredible performance put on by this new Research Chemist in Standard Oil Laboratories in the Bay Area, and so I was thinking – Boy, my honor is saved at least – and just then Charmy opens the door and she says, "Don, Baba is ready for you."

I followed her down the steps. It was a beautiful apartment they had just at the side of Central Park (not looking on the park, but a side street) a lovely one with a living room, with great vaulted two story ceilings and then over in the side of that a jewel, a gem of a little library that, strangely enough, opened with two doors. I think Murshida Duce had exercised some of her greatest decorating instincts on that little library, it was beautiful, absolutely stunning. She was a woman of tremendous taste.

I knew where I was going. Charmy opened the doors. There I saw a chaise-longue she had gotten from somewhere, with the upper part of it (the back part of it) towards the door, and propped up on it was obviously Meher Baba with his leg laid out like this {Don elaborated in person, left leg elongated on the chaise-longue and the other leg down with the foot on the floor} and I took this in quickly. The other part I saw quickly was something ... You know what the air conditioning system was? This was back in the early 1950s, a little bit of air conditioning was around, but the Duces didn't have it in their apartment, so it was a hellishly hot, humid August day. If you've ever been in New York or Washington, DC in August you know what that can be and it's hell on wheels ... no question.

So what they had gotten was one of these old tin washing tubs, you know, that mother used to do her laundry in with a scrub board down in it, if you lived that long ago. I certainly did. So, here is the tin washing tub, with a block of ice in it, with a fan just on the other side blowing across the block of ice onto Baba, to cool Baba. Wasn't it marvelous? Even I was a little bit ashamed of us at that point. Then, in back of the block of ice (on the street side just in front of the windows) were obviously four Indian gentlemen – four of the Mandali, I said to myself, who were traveling with Baba then. I think Sarosh was one of them, Eruch was not in on that particular trip, I believe Meherjee was there, certainly Gustadji was there. [Gustadji] adopted me on the spot, I found that out, pushing and pulling me around right next to Baba's feet from that point on.

Here were the four Mandali, and they were beaming and smiling. Just as soon as the door opened I took all of this in, in one second. That was a still-film that stays with me forever & ever.

As soon as I am in there, immediately Baba on his chaise-longue does this:

{Don explains that Baba used his left hand on the arm of the chaise-longue in back of him to brace himself and started to pivot himself towards the right and off of the couch, so that he could stand with support and then face Don.}

You know, if you've got your leg in a plaster cast and you've got a number of things broken up in your body you don't move terribly well. I saw him turning, and that shocked me first of all (that he would go to all that trouble) and I was just feeling terribly bad, and he just put his right foot definitely on the floor and then began to lower the left in the plaster cast to the floor as well.

Then I knew what he was up to. *I couldn't believe it. He wanted to rise to greet me standing. Can you imagine? Can you imagine.* It shocks me to this day right down to my bones to think of the Avatar doing something like that, any human being doing something like that. And so, I became vocal, immediately. I said, "No, no, no, no! Baba, no, no, no, not that..." And so, Baba turns his head full towards me, smiles, and motions with his hand towards these four men over there, and I saw that was my answer, "Don, I'm going to do what I want to do, and get out of my way." He didn't put it like that, but I saw that was the decision and there was nothing that I could do about it. So a couple of them quickly spring over, and one gets under one arm and the other under the other arm and as quickly as you can say, "Jack Robinson," Baba was on his feet and facing me. And right at his side, completely unruffled by all of this, was Murshida Duce. So I come up a little closer to where Baba is standing, and you know this famous statement (I guess this one has gone around the world a few times) Murshida Duce says, "Baba, this is my boy Don." And Baba, just as fast and as calmly, wiggles his fingers, and it is interpreted, "Your boy? He's not your boy, he's my boy! We've been together since the dawn of time."

Golly that was, you know, he certainly is not backwards about putting ownership where it belongs, is he? He got the priorities right-straight there, right in the first instant and Murshida Duce lived by it from that day on. And it was very obvious that she recognized that Don was Baba's boy. I still worked like a slave for Sufism for her, but nevertheless, that was where the lifeline was.

Now we get into the part where this great repartee is supposed to go on between Don, one of the shining lights of the Sufism Reoriented Order, and Baba. And I didn't know what to say. I was so flabbergasted by Baba's standing there, and saying what he had just said, you know, this was too much to take in. So I simply said nothing at all. Baba looks at me brightly and wiggles his fingers and says, "Did you have a good plane ride out from San Francisco?" and I think I got out, "Uh." That was the extent of my vocalistics. {laughter}

So, anyway, and then I guess Baba felt I wasn't going to add on to that "Uh" and so he wiggles his fingers again and out comes a little bit more, "Are you tired after all of that long journey?" or something ... "Uh." {laughter} And so, you know, another question. {laughter} "Uh."

I couldn't even say "yes," or "no," it was too much. Vocalizing? I wasn't capable of it. I was just absolutely speechless, but my inside was not speechless, not at all. And you know what it said to me? I remember the words instantly, "Don, this man knows you completely, better than you know yourself." You know what I said back? "Uh."

And so, then, the little voice, just like Baba, you know, not to be put off, goes on and says, "And do you know, he accepts you totally."

That was something that had never happened to me in my life, and I had always looked for. And when you find it, you know it, and it's real. So, you see, the central pillar is already in right there. It wasn't Baba saying it, it was myself saying it to me. I'm not a psychic person, I don't have experiences like that, but I knew it. It was a wonderful feeling.

Baba might have said one or two other things, while the inner-man was telling me what the score really was. I have no recollection of what went on. All I know is that for somewhere around ten to fifteen minutes, that Avatar, who's got to put up with these things with us, stood there with his

Don clarified on May 31, 2003 in person to Laurent through dictation, "The inner voice, was 'the little man inside' it was vocal, not an intuitive sense. In an intuitive sense, I've got to supply the words, but I know what words to supply, but this was vocal with words that I was not controlling." Laurent just read that back to Don, and he said, 'precisely correct.'"

busted leg in a cast, you know, smiling and gesturing and people reading his gestures, and Don with his magnificently voluble replies to him, and then Baba said, "Now, Don, we won't have much time further today because I've got some other people I've got to see, and we are going to be together tomorrow, that will be out at Harmon, so I look forward to see you then. We will talk about various Sufi matters…" and so on. And so I didn't even say "Huh," I just turned around and went out, and got out into the lovely great big living room.

I'm sorry this is taking so much time. We are going to spend the whole morning on my fifteen minutes with Baba. I am sorry but I have to do it this way.

Lol Benbow: That physical contact. Baba didn't shake hands or touch you or anything?

Don: He touched nothing at all. It's funny, it didn't run through my mind one way or another. I didn't have any sense of wanting to be closer to him, far away, touching him, anything of the sort. Just being in his presence … and knowing these things inside of me, that was all that was necessary, that was value beyond anything I could imagine.

So I go out into the living room, and there were five, six, I don't know, people sitting around out there waiting to meet Baba. See, all of these fifteen minutes of erudite exchange, kept some people waiting. And I didn't know what to do … Is there a word in the English language (in England) called "pole-axed"? Pole-axe is what you do to a steer when you want to kill it. That's a pole-axe. I was pole-axed. Absolutely, totally.

I saw an empty chair sitting against the far wall, and I went over there and I sat in it. I didn't know what I was going to do while I was doing it, but people went in and out of the little library where we were, and suddenly, my stomach said, "Don, you're neglecting me." I couldn't see how my stomach could get through to me under these circumstances but it sure did. So I looked at my watch and it said somewhere around noon time, and because I hadn't had anything at all to eat (except for a little bite on the plane many hours before) and because I've got good habits of health bred into me by my mother, I said, "I'd better feed my stomach." I went and bought a couple of sandwiches and I came back, I don't know, maybe it was two o'clock by that time. I wasn't going to see Baba, and I didn't know what else to do. I rang the bell and Charmy let me in again, and she knew I was still pole-axed, so she didn't try any conversation. I just went over to my chair and sat down in it, and time moves along and nothing rational went through my mind. *I was just living, just living in Baba at the moment, nothing else, I can't explain it any other way.*

Eventually-suddenly, Filis Frederick, lovely Filis Frederick (who is gone now too) opened the door and said, "Baba's going to tell us a story."

Now I knew why I was there. This was unexpected. You know, this is real frosting on the cake. Or whatever it was. So, I think there was ... John?

John Horder: Was she the editor of the *Awakener*?

¶ Don: Yes. She was living in New York, working for the toy company there at the time, and then moved out to the West Coast, to Los Angeles. After Jack Small came over to the Trust working for Adi Sr., Filis went out and became more or less the head of the Los Angeles group, until her death eventually, not terribly long ago. She was quite an elderly lady, and her old friend Adele Wolkin. There were three of them who were almost always together. And Beryl Williams, the Negro girl, a marvelous person. I wish you could have seen [Beryl] walking in Baba's footsteps, walking from the Barn to the Old Kitchen at Myrtle Beach, one step right after the other, Baba walking in front, and Beryl Williams walking (leaning almost to the ground) right in his footsteps. At any rate, there we are, and Filis opens the door and says, "Baba's going to tell us a story." There we are, marvelous.

Baba is right there, facing to the window, and there is the air conditioning system still going. I don't think there was a block of ice left in it, I don't think there was anything left in it, even the water had evaporated by that time. So here we are, and the first person in goes way around by this [semi-circle] in front of him, a little bit over to the left, and close to the wall, and then ten or fifteen others. I was a very shy person in those days, so I was the last person into the room, and I sat way over around back behind Baba's head. It didn't bother me. I couldn't care less whether I was in front of him, behind him, back beside him or whatever, it made absolutely no difference. You know when there is real, real "humanness," it doesn't matter where you are oriented in relation to it.

There we are, all sort of squatting on the floor there around him and he begins telling his story.

When he was not just conversing, but telling a story (his gestures were always beautiful), but when he was telling a story of some sort or another, which I understood later from Murshida Duce, his gestures were so beautiful, so delicate, incredible motion.

I was absolutely caught up in the beauty of the movements that he was making. I didn't hear a word of the translations of his gestures. I didn't even try. I didn't feel I was shirking my duty, I thought I was watching the most beautiful physical activity I had ever seen in all of my life. I have never seen a ballet dancer, or an oriental dancer, who could approach the beauty and the delicacy of Baba's movements. They were spot on. It wasn't so much that they were delicate, but they were so graceful and harmonious. Incredible. So here I was, and just being completely wrapped up in it.

I am not a terribly demonstrative person, and certainly in that time in my life before I got a little cracked up, I was much less so.

Nonetheless, as I was watching all of this I found myself inexplicably, without willing it at all, raising my right hand, like this, making the circle of perfection, in back of Baba. It was so beautiful. I just don't do things like that, but I did it. It was the only thing that could respond to that sort of beauty, and as I did this, here's Baba and he's gesturing this way and gesturing that way and without pausing he leans on the back of the chaise-longue, and does that {Don makes the gesture circle of perfection} back to me, just as I do it to him. Well, of course, that sort of response and sensitivity, it pole-axed me again. So here I was completely double *non-compos mentis*. I hope we have Latin translators in here, it means I didn't have any mind left. I hope.

At any rate, I was just sitting there and feeling all warm, and Baba was going on telling his story, and telling his story. Remember, it was not too terribly long before that when I had been in a very good university, John's Hopkins University, as a science major and a mathematics minor, and mathematical probability was one of my favorite subjects. So, all of a sudden, the little worm up in the head starts wiggling around and I said to myself – God, the chances of that coincidence happening are one in billion – or something like that. This is absolutely incredible. See, I'm looking at mathematical probability. Miracles or anything like that, you know, I don't even think of such things. I was looking at it from Reality's standpoint.

And of course, Reality says that if a terribly unusual thing happens, and then there is a similar repetition, the chances that two happen in a row is the multiplication of those two improbabilities, meaning zero, zero, zero. My sense of mathematical probability had to get busy moving and see what all this meant. So, I said – I've got no choice, I've got to do it again – I waited until Baba was looking way over at this person (way over at the end up there you see) and when he was the farthest away he could get his eyes from me, I started to get this hand making another perfect circle delicately, rather low down, you see, very low down in front of me. And just as soon as I start doing it, what does poor Baba do? You see, he braces himself on his chair, and turns, smiles and does it back to me. Well, there is mathematical probability, but boy I got a real bonus of feeling out of that one because it was such a beautiful smile he gave me. It was terrific.

There we are, two of them. Well, you would think that ought to be enough, we ought to finish up the day and pack off, and see him the next day and discuss finances and so on, but I'm a little bit of a shaker and a doer, too, you see. When I get started I usually shake things up thoroughly, and get them done thoroughly, Laurent, like you do.

Anyway, here we are. So, after the story is done everyone has to go out, and I go back to my favorite chair and I'm sitting there, doing mathematical probabilities, and – wasn't that a lovely smile – and so on, and so on. I think I was into this for another hour, hour & a half, and the door opened to the library, & Filis says, "Baba's going home now."

Somebody, I guess it was Sarosh, came in from the far side, and he was rolling in front of him (I have never seen anything like it) a collapsible wooden wheelchair. Did you ever see a collapsible wooden wheelchair? I think it was probably invented and manufactured for Noah's ark, it had been sitting around that long. So here comes the wheelchair and I said, "My God, what a thing to get Baba into."

Anyway, Sarosh goes in and starts rolling Baba out the door after about five minutes. Sarosh (if you've never met him) well you take Laurent here, and multiply him about 50 per cent (and more) and stand him up, and that's Sarosh. You see, not a feeble little guy, and tall. And here is the wooden wheelchair, it's about

DES clarifies "At that time, Baba was staying at a rented home, at Harmon-on-Hudson, some miles up the Hudson river."

half as wide as Sarosh is, and Baba is all sort of squeezed up in it. Baba wasn't heavy at all in those days, he was quite slender (and especially after all this accident business) but even Baba was sort of bunched into the little wheelchair. And here's Sarosh, beaming, and rolling Baba out towards the door.

You're going to hate me for this! {laughter} What did I have to do at that point? *What Baba puts up with us, you know, it is absolutely incredible.* I found myself (I did not will this) I found myself going around in back of Sarosh, man-mountain Sarosh, mayor of Ahmednagar (and you could see he could knock the whole town into line if they ever got out of line, Sarosh was like that, a terrific man). He is wheeling Baba along, and here's Don (I wasn't terribly big at that point, I hadn't put on my stomach yet at that point) so I'm just almost crouching behind Sarosh, following right along. Of course, I raise my hand for the third time, down behind the small of Sarosh's back (couldn't have been better) but what happens? Here's poor Baba, all bunched up in this little wooden wheelchair, rolling along. {Don demonstrates how Baba's arms are folded in on his chest}

Baba first of all gets one hand up on the almost non-existent little wooden arm-rest, and pulls on that, and then he pushes on the other arm-rest with his other hand. I've got to groan, just thinking of what he went through. {Don continues to illustrate the painful manner in which Baba positioned himself in the cramped wheelchair to turn, and then Don groans loudly}

He didn't say anything, of course, but I did, and he turns around with that rhapsodic smile and looks at me and makes the sign of perfection again and thereupon settles back and Sarosh rolls him out and they go home.

Well, that was an experience. The reason that I tell you all of this is because certainly Baba knew ... well, he knew who I was, he knows who Baba is, he knew the things that had to be done, and he knew the basis that had to be formed to build them, as this was of course the foundation that was to last my needs on the Path for a life-time. But it was also the base for a tremendous amount of work that had to get done on Baba's words, which we then started to plunge into.

Should we take just about two, three, four minutes, stretch our legs or something, come back, sit down and then we'll polish off this business of the three major assignments for getting what Baba wanted done … started on his words?

⬥

Don : we began a bit differently today from what I had planned originally. I was going to start with one of my morning intuitions that seemed to be aimed directly at this project we are doing together this weekend. I don't know why I changed my mind. Instead, I just thought – no, I am going to start historically, and then when we get into the part about Baba's Word, then we will do this morning's intuition – This was very important to me, because I've gotten tremendously involved with intuition through the years, both in business and also in relation to Baba activities. In recent times there have been a number of people who have become deeply interested in the Avataric gift of intuition, so it has been very much up front and center.

I've noticed over a period, especially in the last two to three years, that very frequently at three thirty in the morning (not the most convenient time) all of sudden, usually when I am coming back from the bathroom (which usually isn't convenient either, but there we are) all of a sudden something that I hadn't thought of springs into my head, terribly strong and clearly. I've made a rule for myself when this happens, to make notes immediately. Then, if I can go back to sleep (which I usually do) then during the course of the twenty four hours, I go back to those notes and write up fully whatever comes through at that point.

I've found that the original intuition itself is sort of like a skeleton. It is bare bones material, and when I go back later in the day to write it up on the computer there is a lot of additional and sometimes very important stuff. Either I was just too fatigued earlier, or else it was too much overloading for that early in the morning.

Now I want to tell you about one other thing that's happened to me since Baba dropped the body. As I mentioned before, I am not a psychic person. I don't have psychic experiences. I do have intuitions, some hunches, things of that sort, but like everybody's. *But there have been two or three occasions, since Baba has dropped the body, when I was in a very distressing personal situation, when all of a sudden it was as if words formed in the back of my head, very simply, clearly and distinctly. On each occasion these words came so much in the manner that I had become accustomed to with Baba, that I immediately said to myself: Baba's telling me something.*

I don't depend on this type of happening, but it has occurred now three times, & the last paragraph of what I want to read to you is the third time that occurred. Now, pin whatever glory trappings you want onto it, or tell yourself that Stevens is being sentimental or imbecilic again, or whatever you want to, but I will read it out to you as the intuition came. This was only a very few days ago. {Don reads aloud a document, quoted below, and makes spontaneous comments on it while reading.}

A Word Before We Start
My job is to tell you what Baba told me about his manifesting;

❡ Don: This comes into it.

... the Path of Love;

❡ Don: He said a lot to me about it.

About the balance of head and heart, Don clarified through dictation in Dijon, France on June 3, 2003, at 7:04 PM to Laurent Weichberger in person, "I realized in recent months that despite my lack of interest in whether I had close to a perfect balance of such important characteristics, that Baba was establishing a key memory within me. This was that he considered such a balance to be important and that he knew that I would remember these two occasions later, that he had emphasized the importance of such a balance. This became clear to me when I saw a very great tendency among his devotees to give great importance to one of the characteristics and to under-evaluate or even to negate the value of the other. End of story. Does that make sense?"

... the balance of head and heart & Don's 'almost perfect balance between the two;'

❡ Don: I wondered why, on two occasions, he buttered me up to tell me something that meant nothing to me, frankly. I don't know whether my heart & head are balanced or not, but he thought it was important enough to bring it up twice, & I have realized since then why he did it ...

... the gradual narrowing of the Path of Love; the role of his words; and the reason for all the Discourses on Meditation.

❡ Don: These are all very important things, and Baba said very clearly and distinctly, at length, many things on all of these. So, it's time to bring them together under one roof now.

If I cannot tell you what he told me, and what he told me it was my responsibility to tell his lovers,

❡ Don: He said that, "It's your responsibility to tell this to my lovers."

... then I will have failed my Beloved.

The story of the three bridges is my observation of how Baba ordered all this within our reference of time and space. I will describe this scenario now, but first, a simple recap of the larger picture I make out of what Baba has provided for us.

❡ Don: Now, I've never put these words together, and they were a surprise to me, but I loved them as they came along. But this part is not what I felt was something coming from Baba direct.

Meditation is the frame in the future within which Baba's gift of intuition to us will operate. And truing of this intuition is the contribution of the head and of the companions bound by inner links. God Speaks *is the great treasure by which intuition, within the frame of meditation, can unearth the riches of the Path.*

❡ Don: And now this next part I put in quotes, because this is the third time in my life I had the distinct feeling this had to be direct from Baba. Everything fitted in.

"Read my words with your hearts open. Use the techniques of meditation I have given you for the frame of intuition for the spiritual charge I have attached to my words to flow into your being. After that, be content that I am one within you and will guide you on the course of your life."

According to Don, this is the third time in his life, after Baba dropped his body, that he had the distinct feeling the intuition had to be direct from Baba. Later in Chapter Three of this volume Don describes this event, "… words formed in my mind when I was doing some intuitive work."

❡ Don: Those are pretty powerful words. Anyway, that's what we have to try to do today. {To John} John, what would you like to say?

John: Is it "special" charge, or "spiritual" charge?

❡ Don: Let's see what I put in …

Norah: "Spiritual charge."

❡ Don: Um-hmm, yeah, "for the spiritual charge …"

When Baba, you remember, talked about the work he was doing with the words he had given in the special manner, he said, "I have attached," something like, "a bomb, an atomic bomb of psychic …" he used in that case, which I simply interpreted as "spiritual" energy, for our spiritual path.

❡ Don: Frankly, I would hate to try to define what's the difference between what is "psychic" and what is "spiritual." There

About the different words, "psychic" vs. "spiritual" Don clarified on June 3, 2003 at 7:30 PM in Dijon, France to Laurent directly in person through dictation, "I am certain that on different occasions I have used both of these words, namely 'spiritual' and 'psychic' to identify the energy that Baba said he had attached to his words. As I reflect, I am almost certain that the word Eruch gave me from Baba was, 'spiritual', but I cannot pretend to be absolutely certain of this. The important thing, however, is that Baba clearly said that this attached energy would be absorbed by the devotee who worked with his words, and that what he (the devotee) had absorbed would be of the greatest value in his spiritual ongoing. There can be no doubt that this was the important point that Baba was establishing. If I have confused the meaning of psychic and spiritual in this circumstance, I regret my failing, and it reflects simply my own lack of discernment."

are so many words that are loosely used. But at this point, in any case, it was a "psychic energy" charge.

So lets get on, now, into *God Speaks* itself, which was the first great document that he sent to us. We worked, as I said, like slaves during the six weeks that he gave us. This didn't mean that everything was finished then, because it had to go to Dodd, Mead [the publisher] with whom we had been negotiating to take on the publishing job. So there was further work that had to be done that was needed to cover very special sorts of points that Murshida was confused on, or on which I would need some guidance.

These came up in later years when I would be sitting with Baba, because I was not sitting with Baba in India at the time that we were editing. In the later period, however, I was acting at one time as sort of a messenger running back and forth between [Charles] Purdom and Baba. Purdom had come out with his new book, *The God-Man*, which was great. It contained many very important things, including a final chapter which is pretty much Purdom's own interpretation of Baba's words (interpreted into Purdom's own Christian background and upbringing).

This was a very tough bridge to try to make, and there were some points in there which I felt needed to be taken up with Baba in India. Baba did discuss them, because they were all important issues, and they involved variations from what Baba himself had said, so we spent a lot of time on that.

Baba would give me messages to carry back to Purdom, because I was living in England at the time, and I loved Purdom very much. I thought he was a wonderful gentleman, really a splendid, splendid human being, as well as a marvelous scholar. It was a rather painful thing for Purdom when Baba didn't see eye to eye with him about this or that point. But Purdom, bless his heart, he never got upset, annoyed or contentious about any of the things that had to be straightened out. So, one by one, everything was resolved until we got down to "the increase in consciousness" that Purdom stated occurs in the human stage.

Baba, of course, was saying that consciousness is full in the first human incarnation. Eventually Purdom said, "No, Don, I just won't accept that until I am sitting one day at Baba's feet." When I reported this to Baba, he said, "Purdom is confusing awareness with consciousness, and that is why he is confused on this point."

This was not the only point that became of concern to Baba. Somewhere in one of his writings Purdom had said something like, "Of course, we really don't have Baba's real words, they are always said through secretaries, and then they have been edited and recast ... and so we don't really know exactly what Baba really said." This was a very important statement coming from such a distinguished man of letters, not just distinguished in Baba's circles but in literary circles throughout England. Everywhere in the literary world, in fact, Purdom was a well known scholar. So, to have Purdom say, "Well, we really don't know what Baba has said..." was a matter of some real concern.

All this happened when Baba was still in the body.

It was during some of the discussions on this that Baba had Eruch explain to me, twice, the precise manner in which, above all, *God Speaks* was given out by Baba. Baba said, "I give a Mandali the key points that I want to be included, and for *God Speaks*, the [first] eight chapters, I gave that direct to Eruch. Then the

Mandali comes back the next morning, reads out what they had written up in brief notes, and I go over it word by word."

Baba was adamant that this was not a quick, nor a superficial thing that was gone through, it was word by word. And then he would have Eruch tell me the story of how he would correct these special words after he gave up the use of the alphabet board by having Eruch say "a, b, c, d, e, f, g ..." and stop him at the needed letter, thus laboriously spelling out the word in this fashion. "Also, Don, Baba's formal addresses to Baba groups on special occasions are given out the same way." This important addition to his description needs to be carefully borne in mind.

But let us return for a moment to the story of Baba's exchanges with Purdom (with Don acting as the messenger). Baba wanted me to focus on what Purdom had said. Baba was not angry with Purdom, he was not even impatient with Purdom, but he knew that he was correcting something in a clear fashion, as it had to be clarified. Baba would go to extreme lengths to clarify words that might be misunderstood, or were somewhat vague in their connotation. *Baba did this editing work, and explained it to me twice in a fashion that left absolutely no doubts that what Purdom had said, and which has gone around the world, was not correct.*

What Purdom wrote is true of some of Baba's words, but it is not true of things where Baba has left us an indelible record that *this* he gave out first as notes to a Mandali, who wrote it up in full form and brought it back to Baba, and Baba then corrected it. That is the first most important thing that has to be carefully understood. This of course is very, very evident for *God Speaks*: eight chapters are by Baba as he intended them, word for word. [Chapters] nine and ten are written by Eruch.

Baba did *not* say that nine and ten were given initially to Eruch as notes, and Eruch wrote them up. Baba did *not* say – I went over them word by word with Eruch and corrected them in the manner I had told you about – *Baba did not say that*. Now, a lot of people have gotten very annoyed with me because a lot of people love Eruch as I do, and they hate to see any sort of "putting down" or possible devaluation of Eruch's contribution. I will tell you just very simply and honestly that the only thing I take with a grain of salt is the verbiage that Eruch uses when he talks about words "given out to amuse the mind," or "paroxysms of the mind," something like that.

Laurent: "Convulsions."

Don: "Convulsions of the mind." This was the one thing which Eruch contributed which struck false to me. I wrote to Eruch (this was after Baba had dropped the body) and I said, "Eruch, can you tell me if you feel content with those words, because I never heard Baba speak about words in such a derogatory manner." It is true that Baba says that words by themselves will not get you anywhere. But to give it such a derogatory sense.

Eruch wrote back, "Don, all I can tell you is that the pen was mine but the hand was not."

That was the end for Eruch, but even as much as I love Eruch, Eruch was a human being, and right up until the time when we are God Realized, you know, we all have our own subconscious contributions that we cannot refrain from making. This is the message that I am going to harp on again, and again, and again during the two days that we are together. As honest as we can be, as much as we love someone, our unconscious is still there, with its problems, with its knots, and it isn't until our last gasp that the last of them is undone.

One of the most trying things that I ever had to do in my life was to admit to myself, as I got to know the Mandali, that I didn't love all of them. Some of them were "cussed-characters," quite frankly. But some of them were just such absolute jewels of human beings that I adored them. I could also see, because

I was around them in awfully intimate situations many times around Baba (and even very private situations), that even with my "pets," I could tell when they were moving in raw ground in their own unconscious. It was still there.

The most painful thing I think I ever had to do personally, was to sit in New York City in Baba's bedroom when one of his favorite Mandali (whom I knew well, and [who is] one of my favorite human beings) had to do an errand for him [Baba]. There he was, and he would read Baba's gestures to me, because he could do that of course, so in addition to taking the instructions Baba gave of what he had to do, he was translating for me.

Baba wanted him to do a complex series of reservations for travel, so after understanding exactly what Baba wanted him to do, the guy goes out, somebody else comes into the room and I stay on with Baba for awhile. Later in the afternoon I was again in Baba's room. It was not usual for me (or anyone else) to be in Baba's private room. When he received people he was down below. Why I was there, I don't recall. Obviously, to teach me a lesson about Baba's relationship even to his close Mandali.

Then this Mandali came back again, and when he came in he had to announce to Baba that, "Baba, I couldn't do what you asked me to do because of…" this, and that, and the other thing, and still another thing…

For one of the two or three times that I was around Baba [in such a state] I then saw Baba go into an uproar. *He was outraged, and he bawled this person out.* I was cringing, I wanted to crawl under the bed, I wanted to escape, I loved them both. To see this happening was crucifying to me.

Then, you won't believe this. For a third time I was again in Baba's room when this Mandali came back and said, "No, I still haven't been able to…" Another tirade from Baba. – My God – If the first one was tough, the second one was absolutely impos-

sible. I felt the Mandali was going to burst out crying, it was
so crucifying. Baba said – Did you try this, did you try that, did
you try another … – Two times, "no." And so then, later in the
day, he came back. I was still around. I don't know how all this
happened, but I learned my lesson, and he said, "Baba, I did it."
Baba immediately loved him, and fondled him, and so on. And
it was all done.

All this showed me that, even as close as the Mandali are, as
chosen as they are, as close to perfection as they are, they still
have sanskaric knots, as we have, right up until the last, they are
there.

Baba cast a great deal of light on all this for me once when I
had what I had thought was a marvelous idea. I have told many
of you the story, because so many of you have the same problem. After being around Baba for years and seeing the simple,
beautiful life they lead in India, I was ashamed
of Stevens' fat expense account with a big oil   Don Stevens eventually
company and the "life-of-Riley" that I led, prin-   became a Vice President at
cipally on expense account.   Chevron Oil Company

I was expected to lead that sort of life and entertain in that
fashion, great hotels and restaurants, and so on, because I was
an important representative of an important global company.

Finally, I couldn't stand it anymore. I decided I just had to go
back to the university and switch professions and take up Social
Sciences, or something of the sort, and go into something more
closely related to human beings. So I said – I can't do this though
without telling Baba about it – just being sure that he doesn't get
upset or something.

I did not ask Baba for personal instructions in my life, that
was taboo for me, and I think it should be for most people. At
any rate, I didn't. But with this one, I realized that Baba had gotten pretty far into my petroleum life for various reasons, and I

didn't want to upset that course if he felt a change on my part would not work out right. So when I got to India I said – well, the first thing I've got to do is tell Baba about this. Finally, when Baba said, "Now Don, what's been going on, what's happening in your personal life?" I said, "Baba, I have something terribly important I've got to talk over with you." I got as far as saying, "Baba I just feel ashamed of myself when I come over here, and see the simple life that you people lead, and I've got to go back to school …" I don't think I even got the word "school" out of my mouth when all of a sudden Baba looks over at Eruch and wiggles his fingers, and they are in a conversation, and I said – this is a helluva time to have a conversation when I am trying to tell Baba about an earthshaking decision in my personal life – I was upset, quite frankly.

I was trying not to criticize Baba, even quietly to myself, because when I have done that a couple of times, he immediately said, "Don, what are you thinking about?" {audience laughter} So, I didn't go that far, you see. I'd learned my lesson, on that one in any case. On this occasion he is talking with Eruch, back and forth, and so on. And then he said, "Don, what is it you were saying to me?" So I start going back, and I repeat some of the ground I had already covered. But I don't think I even caught up to where I was the first time before he cut me off. He cut me off again, and he and Eruch talked longer this time, and so I said to myself – I'm going to wait until things are more peaceful and then I will bring it up. And of course, I never got to the peaceful bit. Instead, I got on the plane, and then said – Oh my God. I didn't remember to bring that up again with Baba.

A second trip to India. Exactly the same thing happened. You just wouldn't believe it. And I got fed up and said – Well … – And then a third time I came and I said, "Baba this is terribly important, I've got to talk to you about this." This time he stands still for it, and as soon as I say, "I've got to go back to college and do something closer to human beings," he waggles his finger at me and says, "Who do you think got you into Standard Oil of California?"

And he dropped it. *Good heavens, it has to be.*

It just has to be that Baba, Baba knew that karmically that was the fit. And as I know that the Avatar wiggles time and space, so he had wiggled time and space and got me an appointment through a very close sympathetic friend employed in the company and I went into Standard [Oil] of California. *He said, "Yes, it was Baba, and do you know why? Because the environment in the oil industry is exactly what you need for the particular sanskaras which are to be worked on in this lifetime."*

Now that was a whole new concept of sanskaras and how you go about working on them. I had just always assumed – sanskaras pop up, sanskaras pop up – they come up from here, they come up from there, and so on. But no. Baba was saying that it is related to a deliberate choice selection in a certain area of your own background, and others are left untouched, obviously. So he said, "And that is where they will be worked out the best, and so you stick with it."

In other words, the ones that are for this lifetime – stay with them. Don't go flittering off into another field over there. Work the ones through right here.

That's what I call (Stevens has to put a mechanical framework around this) this is what I call the "wedge of sanskaras" approach to living. All right, this lifetime it is *this wedge*, another lifetime it's *another wedge*, another lifetime it's *still another wedge*. So one thing finally made sense that had never made sense before. I've had some really wonderful friends, but I have also on occasion been absolutely shocked to my toe-nails that this wonderful friend that I thought I knew so totally well, when we were in a new territory that we haven't been in together before, I would find this wonderful friend acting like a savage.

I would say – but how can this possibly be true? And for the first time in my life it came to my realization that we can have spent a lot of time on a number of sanskaric wedges, but then, when in one way or another life leads us over into another wedge that we haven't spent perhaps any time on, working deeply and honestly, and de-energizing and so on, we are like savages, and I am like a savage. Moreover, this is the only thing that has explained to me certain things that I have noted even in the Mandali. All of this said to me that even the Mandali still have wedges. Now I think, if you follow Bhau's – what does he call them?

Female participant: "Awakenings."

¶ Don: Awakenings. Bhau's Awakenings. He had, I thought, an absolutely beautiful one on this, in which he gave the example of how Baba worked on the Mandali's sanskaras. And he gave some incidents that came up in relation to [William] Donkin and how Baba crucified Donkin on diet at one point. And I said, "Well, Bhau, you have done a tremendous service in pointing out to people how Baba himself worked on eliminating the Mandali's sanskaras, because they will listen to you on this, this is your experience, and you are a close Mandali."

I thought Bhau did a marvelous service to humanity in verifying that even the close Mandali have got chunks of their nature on which the Avatar is still working. This is also part of what we are going to be going back and forth on together during this weekend. I have had to admit to myself that the one thing we have in our spiritual heritage that is absolutely dependable is Baba's carefully given out and corrected words. From there we get into all sorts of other areas of contribution, and sometimes even from good Mandali, close Mandali. But we cannot give them the same attribution of value that we do to Baba's own words. There is a vast difference.

It was about then [during the 1950s] that another terribly important conversation came along, after we got through [the publishing of] *God Speaks* and the backs-and-forths, comments and footnotes, and so on. But first, remember this above all, that the first eight chapters of *God Speaks* are Baba, and that he carefully, carefully, carefully had Eruch explain to me exactly how he gave those [chapters] to Eruch. Then they were carefully corrected. [Chapters] nine and ten are Eruch. Almost all of the Supplement is [Dr.] Ghani. And you remember probably the story …

Baba recounted to us with no animosity at all, how he had been giving Ghani notes over quite some months time before he came to America, for a new book. When Ghani had died unexpectedly of a heart attack, and Baba had the material checked over he found that Ghani had written completely different subject matter. But he said to Ivy, "Now a lot of good Sufi material is in that, because Ghani was a very fine Sufi, and you being the head of the Sufi Order, you may want to save part of it. Or, you can even save all of it, or maybe none of it, to go in with the material I gave out for *God Speaks*. I give you the choice."

So Ivy Duce, because of her deep, deep interest and knowledge of Sufi lore, gave her decision back to Baba that she wanted to keep it all. But I know of absolutely nothing anywhere that says Baba went carefully over and corrected the material. He was ready to toss it in the ash-can, totally. I loved Ghani also by the way, so please don't assume I feel any animosity towards him. But the *Supplement* was due to go into the trash-bin as far as Baba was concerned, except he thought it might be of interest to Murshida Duce. Now we get onto some very, very delicate ground. Many people feel, and I understand the feeling, that Baba would never allow a book to come out, above all *God Speaks* by Meher Baba, unless it had his complete stamp of approval. End of story.

Well, it had his approval, but it did not say that all of the words were vetted by Baba. This is the thing that we have to be careful of as we start passing on into future generations Baba's word. The ones that I know myself to have had his careful personal vetting are based principally on my own conversations with Baba, and also Eruch. In one unusual and important case, however, that of the composition of the *Song of the New Life*, the key details were furnished by Adi Irani Sr. (Baba's secretary for so many years). What I know from Baba's explanations to me, the works that are absolutely irrefutably Baba's and also corrected by Baba in the minute manner he had Eruch describe to me twice are the first eight chapters of *God Speaks*, Part II of *Listen, Humanity*, and through Adi Sr., the *Song of the New Life*. [The "Song" is not to be confused with Baba's arresting comments to the public at the end of the New Life that "... this New Life is endless and even after my physical death it will be kept alive by those who ..."]

Baba gave the original notes for the song to Ghani, giving rise to the confusion by which many people say it was Ghani who did the *Song of the New Life*. But it came from Baba, and after Ghani had gotten it written up and corrected by Baba, then Baba had him send it to Adi Sr. to print.

Adi Sr. told me the exact history from that point. He said, "This is the only thing that Baba asked me twice to send to him for re-correction." After the original Baba-corrected Ghani material was sent to Adi, it went to the printer. It was sent back to Baba to correct again, back to Ghani, and then Ghani made some further ones, and then back to Baba for a final correction.

In addition to the very special works I have just described, I have to tell you very, very simply – and I am talking as a human being now – I love the *Discourses* very deeply, very deeply. To me they are very special, to me like the "Bible of Daily Life." And I worked a long time, again under Baba's direction, on those.

It was during the time of working on them that two terribly important things happened, so I will break right in here and tell you about them now.

When I got about half, maybe two thirds, of the way through the work on the original Deshmukh edition of the *Discourses*, I was struck by the fact that Baba gave more discourses on meditation than any other subject. *More on meditation.* And when I started to think about that I thought – Gee, this is absolutely crazy, because when I was a Sufi and I was just starting to get to the point where Murshida Martin was giving me simple meditations and concentrations, Baba took over, and Baba sent her instructions at once to stop all exercises on meditations and concentrations.

I thought – Gee whiz, how come this sort of attitude on what has been a pillar of mysticism for thousands of years? Meditation, after all. And Baba stops it, and here am I left.

Now, as I was going through editing the Deshmukh edition I said to myself – Golly, something's screwed up here. Really crazy. How come Baba gives more discourses on meditation than any other subject, and yet he stopped us on meditations when I was under Murshida Martin. And he's never given me one since then. He must have lost his mind. He's not paying proper attention to good old Don Stevens who is working like a slave on all of these things – So I decided I was just going to have this out with Baba.

Each time I arrived in India Baba would ask, "How are things coming along, how are you getting on?" So the next visit I paid I said, "Well, Baba, frankly I've got something that confused me and it bothers me, and I've got to straighten it out with you. How come so many meditation discourses, and yet you stopped us on it when we became Sufism Reoriented, and you've still never given me one?"

No sooner said, than the little voice inside said, "I'm treading on terribly dangerous ground here. I wonder whether I'll get the whiplash this time."

Instead Baba said, "Good question, Don." {Don makes a big sigh} Sigh of relief.

He said, "Don …" And this is a terribly important point, note the word "Manifestation" … *"Baba says to you that during the period of his Manifestation, and for some time afterwards, the Path of Love, which is the highroad of all roads to Realization, is fully opened to all of humanity. But gradually, the Path of Love will slowly narrow, and finally will be inaccessible to all but a very small percentage of devotees. Then, the second major road, not as great as love, but the second major road to Realization will have to be used and that is meditation."*

Do you realize that first of all Baba is simply saying that, yes, love is terrific. He explained to me that love, of all human qualities, can marshal and focus better than any other human quality, the psychic energy to do the job. Love. But then he went on to say, "But the Path of Love will gradually narrow, and then meditation, the best of the secondary roads, will be used."

I must say, even the very few Mandali to whom I mentioned what Baba had said were shocked to pieces and they regurgitated it. Really, they could not accept it. They said, "Don, Baba has emphasized to us so much, so many times, love, the importance of love, and the utilization of love, and we just know that it is open eternally now."

But how can that be true if Baba himself told me that, "No, the path of love will gradually - the gate - will gradually narrow, and it will become all but inaccessible, and then meditation…" That's exactly what he said to me.

Then he went on, *"Don, I have to prepare for the next seven hundred years, so I have to plan for the time when meditation must be used before I come again."* That means that the Path of Love is going to become relatively inaccessible, not maybe before four or five hundred years from now, but pretty damn soon. We've got to be realistic. These are things that I just had to tell you, and if you say, "Don, some way you've got to be nuts!" or better more like Purdom. Purdom didn't say, "Don is nuts," but, "Something's screwed up here and I won't believe it until I hear it directly from Baba."

{Don addresses a female in the audience}

Don: Kavita, what would you say?

Kavita: Well, I'm finding it hard to accept as well.

Don: I am sure you would. Go ahead.

Kavita: Well, is there any other story or example where Baba said the same thing to somebody else?

Don: I don't know of anyone except Don Stevens who is telling this story exactly as Baba gave it to him. That's the blunt truth. There's been no repetition of it from all I know.

Another Female Participant: ... [that thing is] linked to his Manifestation of the next hundred years, and dropping his body, is the only way I can understand it.

Don: We're not finished yet. There is another very important & tough observation to be made. And none of the Mandali could accept this either. The automatic outcome of what he had just said was – I have already Manifested and that is why the Path of Love is fully open to you. This is why I have not given you meditation.

I can only tell it exactly as it was said and the inevitable conclusion I drew from the clear sequence, and that was he had not given Don a meditation as Don had come under his direct charge after Baba had already manifested, and further I had never known him to give another devotee a meditation in this or subsequent periods, and still further when I tested my own inner experience of giving a shove to all Creation as part of his Manifestation I felt clearly this had happened in the early to mid-sixties.
— Don Stevens

Alright, if the Path of Love is fully open only when he has

manifested, as he had just clearly said to me, it meant he had already manifested and I took that as Gospel Truth. It wasn't until some of the Mandali would come out vociferously, that "No, Baba hasn't manifested …" and it will probably be such-and-such a period of time before he does … or some people even put specific numbers to how many years after dropping the body he would manifest. I must be honest with you. {To Laurent } Yes?

Laurent: I just wanted to say one thing, that I do remember one story of someone asking Baba if they could meditate in his physical presence, and that he basically said something like – Why? If you are in my physical presence there is no need to meditate – And he went on, & if I remember it correctly he explained something, maybe just touched upon the fact that now the Path of Love is there, and make the best use of that, and hinted at that it won't always be that way.

¶ Don: Yes.

Laurent: So I think somewhere in the literature there is something about it, but finding it of course is another story.

¶ Don: Anyway. I had never seen words from Baba, in print, which simply put what Baba told me clearly and indelibly on that day, with Eruch translating his gestures. It was so clear, and it was so vital to him. He sat me down and gave me that lecture. But I have not argued with the Mandali about Baba's Manifesting either. To me he Manifested. I know it. John?

John: Can we just very briefly touch on the supplement [to *God Speaks*]? That meant that Ghani wrote the "forgetfulness" section?

¶ Don: I think that's one of the most beautiful things in Baba literature, John.

John: So do I.

¶ Don: This is Ghani.

John: This is Ghani?

¶ Don: That is Ghani.

John: It's astonishing.

¶ Don: Well, he was a pretty bright guy, and he loved Baba deeply. As far as I can see he just got an awful lot of things right. I mean they harmonize with things I also got direct from Baba.

John: But I mean it is a complete jewel.

¶ Don: It is a complete jewel, one of the most beautiful ones I know. Renate, you're about to say something?

Renate: Exactly, I was thinking about what a shock it is that the [gate to the] Path of Love will decrease as the road to God. Think about it, maybe we don't know actually *what that kind of love is*. Because, you know, what is [in all of us] and will stay, there is no doubt about it, is that love is one of the most important qualities. I would say divine qualities in man. So because…

¶ Don: Thank God we got on the train while it was still around.

Renate: Yes, and because it's this old, old memory of Oneness which is reflected in that capability, so that memory of Oneness is … {Renate makes a big sigh} …what drives us on to God. So that will never go. That will never go. But what it is, is that there seems to be something else he has designed as the road to God. I mean there is of course the other record of what …

¶ Don: Tomorrow we are going to go into that, and maybe some other things that are going to be terribly important.

Renate: What we said about intuition … and I wouldn't say intuition is or is not about love. It is, and you will talk about it, but I think it's that fear that our concept of love is suddenly rocked here by saying that it may not be the main tool … because we are very, very conditioned … what love is … it is the best, the most da-da-da-da …

¶ Don: Renate. Excuse me Renate, it is not the quality, but the availability of access to the Path of Love. Availability. Baba was simply saying – … and it will not be as available. A hero will still be able to use it, but to the average humanity, no – Just simply in those words, it's the availability. Nothing is happening to the quality of love itself.

{background discussion among the audience}

Norah: The quality is not altered?

¶ Don: The quality is not altered, it is simply: how available is the Path of Love later in the Avataric Period? How can you unlock the door, getting in on the Path of Love. How do you get through the gate, if the gate has gotten terribly narrowed? Baba – I always used the term, in my mind – he gave me the sense that a hero on the path will be able to get through, but you have to be a pretty top-notch hero for that to happen.

Kavita: …just reminded me that, a couple of weeks ago, I read that meditation, when you repeat Baba's name, or God's name, is a two fold thing. It's repeating God's name but it's also knocking on the door for his love. I just thought of that.

¶ Don: And sometimes maybe you have to knock a little harder, and a little harder, and a little harder. Baba did not say [the Path of Love] would be unavailable. Wayne?

Wayne Smith: I am not familiar with the discourses on meditation … There's a difference between the Path of Love, and using love as a practice, which will probably still be there in the future.

¶ Don: But of course he certainly does give a powerful discourse on love itself centrally, with a lot of things that nobody ever bothers to read in it, I find. Excuse me, I'm "sour-grapesing," I know. {laughter}

¶ Don: {to Laurent} Did you have something?

Laurent: Just a tiny thing to add. I always got the feeling from what you were saying, Don, that Baba was talking about *the love that he's giving now as the Avatar*, and that is felt so widely by humanity, would be a different experience, in the future, for people. And that most likely, we have no idea how good we've got it with his love, and people in the future will look back on us and say, "Look how lucky they were, they had no idea how much love they got."

Don: And that's true, and it's absolutely true.

Norah: The concept of "God is Love" very much came with the Christian message, wasn't it?

Don: I think we'll go into this a-lot-lot more, too. {To a participant} What would you add?

Participant: I was thinking about the different rays, and energetically there's different eras and times for a different dispensation or push in different rays, and this feels like the push of the Ray of Love, and there will be a different push in a different way, in a different time in the future, but nothing diminished by any of that.

Wayne: Do you think, Don, this is the case for all Avataric advents? That there is …

Don: Baba gave it in the context that, "when the Avatar manifests…" These are the words that he used: "When the Avatar manifests, and for some time afterwards, the Path of Love is fully open, but then it gradually narrows and becomes increasingly inaccessible, at which time the best secondary route is that of meditation."

Norah: But he never says why?

Don. Why.

Norah: Why it will narrow.

Don: Why it will narrow? You know {laughs}, I would like to hear you speculate on this, Norah, because if anybody can speculate on this one it's…

Norah: I'm not going to speculate on anything. But Baba never actually said, I don't think, why.

Don: No, he certainly did not.

Participant: Could I just say something? I have always felt that the way that Baba-lovers use all their love for Baba, that putting their attention on him, that that actually is a meditation and that I think in future probably it will be accepted as a meditation, whereas now Baba-lovers don't think that that is what it is. They just think that it's love.

¶ Don: Yes. But it may be in the future that, let's say, you use as a meditation love of Baba, but Baba was implying that meditation is very much less effective [now] than simply expressed love is now. This is the simple blunt fact. Norah, I wanted to ask you for a moment. I've been talking about things that Baba stamped as having these [energy characteristics of his] very special words, this very special spiritual energy attached to them. You've been around Baba's words quite a bit. Are there some of his writings that especially appeal to you, or have a tremendous vibration within you, as you touch them?

Norah: Well that's difficult, isn't it? Because there is so much. I think I always come back to the chapter in the *Discourses* on love.

¶ Don: That's one of your favorites?

Norah: Yes. There's always something new in it whenever you read it. But there is a bit, I think you put us on to it the other day, about the balance of heart and mind.

¶ Don: Heart and head.

Norah: Yes, heart and head, in that chapter. Which is enormous, really, if you read it. So much in it. And he talks about how the balance works: how it can be the heart and the head working parallel and never ever touching each other, really. There is no cross-fertilization or anything. And then he says there is a period when the head and the heart are at cross purposes and it's all mixed up and you're in a terrible conflict … because your heart interferes with your thinking, and your thinking interferes with your heart. And then he says, that that phase is absolutely essential for reaching the, what comes after, where they are transformed into ...

¶ Don: Super-consciousness, I think.

Norah: Into Real Consciousness, Super-consciousness.

¶ Don: Yes.

Norah: But it struck me that this area, where we are all in (right now) aren't we, where it's absolutely mixed up. And it's very central in achieving that Super-consciousness.

¶ Don: So, "Put up with it."

Norah: That's what has been striking me this last week, I've been thinking about it, yes.

John: Is this Super-consciousness what's been called "DC," Divine Consciousness in the e-mails {from Wayne Smith}?

¶ Don: Now you be careful, Wayne is in the back. {laughter} {much background conversation}

¶ Don: Well, I have no comment on that. Norah I'm awfully glad that you point out that marvelous, marvelous, detailed description of Baba in the discourse on love. Everybody loves to quote the last sentence in that discourse, where Baba simply says, isn't it, that the Creation was created for Love? But they never get back to the more detailed things that Baba goes into fundamentally [on this very important point of the necessary combination of head and heart].

I point out to all of you, if you will look at something that you probably have never even seen – the small section written by Baba himself, at the very beginning of *God Speaks*, I think it's before the *Table of Contents* [p. xxxvi]. Baba is going on about – I have come to do this, and I have come to do that and, "I shall revitalize all religions and cults and bring them together like beads on one string." But then he goes on to say something which I have never heard anybody quote, the next to the last sentence: *"I shall bring about a happy blending of the head and the heart."* There it is, right at the beginning, the very beginning of *God Speaks*, but I've never heard anybody quote that part of it, isn't that amazing? So Baba strings these things about, but someway or another we "edit-in" the things we think are really terrific, and we "edit-out" the ones that are not quite as attractive. 'Cause, lets face it, head has a lousy reputation these days, doesn't it? Should we stop for lunch now?

Aspen: Yeah.

2 : Saturday Afternoon

*W*E STARTED THE SESSION with a viewing of the film of *Meher Baba At Home 1960.* Since Don was actually the cameraman for most of the film he is making spontaneous comments on what we are watching. Baba and Deshmukh are playing seven tiles with the Mandali ...

¶ Don: Here is Baba using Deshmukh as his counterpart for really doing a good "hamming it up." Deshmukh is the fall guy for the Avatar. Finally Deshmukh came up "to bat" again. I mean, actually, to throw the ball, and it was so wild this next time that Baba said, "Deshmukh, for you we halve it." Means, you can go half-way to the tiles. Deshmukh threw again. He completely missed it again {Don laughs to himself} and so Baba said, "We halve it again for you, Deshmukh." And at that point, Deshmukh was almost right vertically over the pile of tiles, dropped the ball, and still missed it. {laughter} Baba was so terribly human. Now, golly, we've got a lot of material to cover this afternoon. There is one other thing that I have to cover. You know, I've been very frank with you about the manner in which *A Word Before We Start* originated, as it was simply an early morning intuition that arrived very soon before this seminar.

But intuition gets to be so – what should I say – almost a regular run, that when something is coming up like this seminar, then intuitions seem to keep popping up all the time. Yesterday, at lunchtime, I was finishing off some rather dry bread and I thought, – Well, I'd better put this in with the new loaf of bread. That way it will pick up some of the moisture from the new bread, and the old stale loaf I can finish eating this evening. – And then, all of a sudden, you know, normally for me intuition works at 3:30 in the morning, and this is the first time that a really rather astonishing sequence rolled out. Part of it, it seemed to me, had so much to do with what we would be doing today, that I said, well I've got to share this with the companions when we're together on the weekend.

Now, I must warn you that the experience ended up being so profound that for at least an hour, when I was trying to write up the event, every time that I thought of it, tears would come to my eyes. So if I touch it, I'm just going to have to lean on my two pillars [Norah and Laurent] and they are just going to have to finish it off for me. I know these are very personal things, but I just feel that we are personally together in Baba's Love. And that's the most personal way of all to be. So let's be personal for a few minutes.

{Don reads a printout of his intuition, shown here in quotes, and comments on what he is reading}

"Time: 13:25 Friday, 2nd May, 2003. Place: Stevens Intuition Command Center."

❝ Don: I hope you like the title.

"This is to report to you the activity on the London intuition front during the last hour."

❝ Don: Are we all settled? So, this was an intuition at lunchtime yesterday. It just seemed to relate, the latter part of it, to the sort of things we are working on today, so I said, obviously this is meant to be shared with the companions when we get together. So, bear with me for a few minutes:

"I was returning things to the kitchen front…"

⁋ Don: "The kitchen front …" You know, this being the Command Center, it means the front line of battle.

"… after a lunch of salad, cheese and wine followed by coffee, but all this transpired as I started to put the remaining stale end of the whole wheat bread into the wrapper with the new loaf just brought home from Safeway's. I enjoy my bread at lunch with the salad and the cheese, but as I eat perhaps three slices at most each day, one loaf lasts several days, and the end left after three or four days is always rather hard."

⁋ Don: I am sure you've had this experience.

"… As I put the old piece into the wrapper containing the newly bought loaf, I told myself as a practical matter, as seems to be my nature - Laurent says I am the most frugal person he has ever encountered, but he says it with great love and no animosity - so, as I was giving Laurent's opinion its due and left the domain of practicality, it crossed my mind that the absorption …"

⁋ Don: {Don looks up from his notes and stares pointedly at the group} I hope you haven't eaten too much, because this is going to tax you.

"… that the absorption of moisture by the stale end loaf from the newly bought bread was due to random motion of molecules of air, including vapor."

⁋ Don: Are we still here? {laughter and assent} OK. {now Don laughing} You see, intuition can be based on rather strange things at times, so here we go.

"… The trick here was that the stale loaf emitted fewer molecules of water vapor than did the new loaf, and so absorbed moisture during the intervening hours. So, it would become far more edible on Saturday, today, when Norah and Laurent were due to share lunch with me after the morning session on Baba's Word and the Three Bridges."

❡ Don: I don't know if they knew they were eating stale bread, but it went down at any rate. There we are. So it would become far more edible on Saturday, which is today.

"... Suddenly, it struck me that this principle of random motion is one of the greatest and least appreciated principles in Creation, allowing the constant progress of drop-souls through the process of duality and the manifesting of latent consciousness."

❡ Don: {reflectively} Don't think that's quite as obvious, but bear with me.

Participant: Could you repeat that?

❡ Don: Yes, um-hmm. {Don repeats the reading of "Suddenly it struck me ..."} Now, comes the explanation.

"... This seems like a tremendous leap from converting stale bread into less stale bread, but as I sat with my coffee, I saw the beginning of the process that had leaped out at me as I put the old bread in the wrapper with the new bread. I think the key is that I feel deeply that as each drop-soul issues from the Om Point, it carries a responsibility for the manifesting of latent consciousness in a particular area of God's Reality."

❡ Don: This goes back two years ago when, you remember, Marion said, "To me Creation is like an enormous jig-saw puzzle as if each drop-soul is responsible for a part, a jig-saw [portion] of that, and that's their domain [in which they develop consciousness]." I thought that was beautiful.

Norah: But your molecules [of water vapour] are interactive, I mean they were ...

❡ Don: Well, now I'm carrying it one stage beyond where Marion was. This is known as creativity. Or further intuition.

"… Also, I am increasingly aware that there has to be a considerable amount of coding …"

Don: Coding. I mean coding is where you put a code number on something and it recognizes the place that it's coded to go to. That is very important.

"… considerable amount of coding that goes on between the drop-soul and Creation, in which the drop soul knows when it is near something that relates to the portion of God's Reality with which it is charged.

"As Creation is so enormous in extent and the drop-soul is enforced to operate within the bounds of this enormity of time and space, it would tax the laws of chance greatly if the drop-soul had to wander about searching endlessly for its area of responsibility, and here is where the principle of random motion comes in."

Don: See, it's going to be explained now.

" The drop soul does not necessarily have to do all the moving, as random motion also provides new resources of environment constantly, and so the problem of being in the right place at the right time is at least halved."

Don: Cut in half.

"Hence, random motion as a natural principle is of great aid to the process of the drop-soul's ability to manifest latent consciousness.

"As I sat down …"

Don: Now here's the part where something new came in and, well, I may get into trouble.

"As I sat down with my coffee and was all but overcome by

such a block-buster intuition having occurred in the middle of the day,"

¶ Don: Instead of 3:30 in the morning, for a change … {which is Don's usual time for the arrival of intuitions}

"… I was swept away then by another, which is so audacious and exciting that it brought tears to my eyes at once by its beauty. Each time I recall it and the wonder with which it swept me, I find tears return."

Norah: Can you say that last sentence again?

¶ Don: Yes {Don repeats the reading from "Each time I recall it …"} And it may be necessary that I stop somewhere about now and put one arm over Norah's shoulder and the other over Laurent's, before I will continue … {hard to hear Don as he starts welling up with tears} It doesn't sound incredible, but…

Norah: {hard to hear her} … a bit about what you were saying this morning about having the sanskaras that we actually, not just any old sanskaras, the ones that have been knocking around, but the ones that we need.

¶ Don: That are right for us here. Yeah, hmm. You see where we are Laurent? {Don indicates that he wants Laurent to continue the reading}

Laurent: Um-hmm {takes the paper from Don and continues to read the intuition}

" … before I will continue with the most desperately incredible thought that has ever swept over my consciousness. It is very simple. What if it is true that the latency of consciousness of God is really undetermined and it is the infinite number of drop-souls who truly and creatively fill in the spaces assigned to them in God's infinitude of consciousness of His own divinity? And what if it is the Whim who is the Leonardo da Vinci of God's consciousness and responsible for getting all the drop-souls onto the proper canvases and the right pieces of marble and palettes of color to create the mastery of God's infinite consciousness? What, in sum, if that consciousness is not latent in either major form or detail, and all this is really being created as it is being experienced in the atelier of Creation? Then, we have some idea of the enormous responsibility to the Father that is that of the Avatar, who oversees all this staggering challenge to creativity within Creation.

As I finish this report to myself on this morning's intuition, I know that it is too big and too important to toss out as a finished or even really well begun work, but I found it so moving that I wanted to contribute it to our sharing of the greatest value we have in our lives, which is the presence among us of the Avatar."

Don: {Turning to Laurent} So, thank you, other pillar. Well, I think, this morning we have gotten up into the beginning of the activity nearing the Discourses. Baba, when we had finished off the editing of *God Speaks* had invited me (I think about a year or two afterwards) to what he called the "Four Language Groups Sahavas." When I had spent the week there with the first group and then had to go back home, he asked me to come around to say goodbye. This was up on the hill at upper Meherabad, and he had on a little table sitting next to his seat a pile of papers.

After he asked me, "How did it go? Did you enjoy yourself?" and so on, he said, "Don, I have here a small collection of addresses that I have given on various public occasions," and he said, "You know all about that." He was referring to the fact that he had told me very carefully that it was his custom when he gave an address at a public occasion, he would do the same thing that he did for *God Speaks:* give certain kernels of ideas to a Mandali, have them bring it back after they had written up the detailed version over-night, and then he would correct this with the Mandali in question.

What he was telling me was that this little pile of papers was given in precisely the same manner that he had given eight chapters of *God Speaks* to Eruch. So that [pile of papers Baba had with him] became then Part II of *Listen, Humanity*. Baba said, "Now if you would like, perhaps, you've done so much work on *God Speaks* that you may not like to take on this further work."

I said, "Good heavens," you know, it was incredible. I was bowled over that he would trust me with it.

Baba said, "You'll find that some of them {indicating the little pile} are one or two pages long, and some of them are only two or three sentences long. But you may find that they do fit together, and that you can do something similar to making a small book of material like the *Discourses* from it."

I said, "Baba, I would love to do this, I will try. I don't know if I am capable of it."

He said, what he always said, "I will help you." Just that simply.

Then he leaned back and said, "In fact, when I think of it, that would be a short book, but you might like to make something a bit longer. For instance, here you've been at part of the sahavas for the language groups, and if you want I will get the transcript of what I have said before them (taken down by two secretaries), brought together, typed up and sent to you and you can make that the heart of another part of such a work." Then he said almost as an after-thought, "And of course the atmosphere, the surroundings, your observation of the people, how they react with each other. Describe that, that would be an important part of that section."

And I said, "Well it sounds like a tremendous idea." That became Part I [of *Listen, Humanity*].

And then he said, "And of course, your own personal thoughts and reactions, you should include that." That became Part III [of *Listen, Humanity*].

When I wrote Part III, I said to myself – My God, when some people read some of the things I've addressed (probably too frankly here) they'll be pretty upset with me – So that was how *Listen, Humanity* came to be written.

I wanted to tell you the whole little story, that it all came directly from Baba. But I do not pretend that anything but Part II is done in exactly the same way as the eight chapters of *God Speaks*, in that meticulous manner. You should know that, and that should be preserved as being an important fact.

Then I had mentioned what Ghani, or rather, Adi Sr. [Adi K. Irani] told me about the background of Baba's giving out the *Song of the New Life*, which I love. I think it's one of the most superb [works from Baba], and I always call it, "incendiarilly revolutionary."

Which I think it is. It says things that I don't think anybody has ever dared say (about the spiritual path) before and I love it. So that also is doubly-doubly not only given out by Baba to a Mandali, but doubly checked by Baba before being sent out.

I've always felt that certainly the two, I think, great prayers, *The Master's Prayer* [O Parvardigar] and the prayer of forgiveness [*Prayer of Repentance*] had to have been given out in the same meticulous manner. The manner that I personally saw Baba use "O Parvardigar" repeatedly, it just has Baba's stamp in a way that I think very few things have.

Then, as I mentioned this morning, to me the *Discourses* are Baba's bible, especially to young people. How to live the spiritual path and the challenges that you find and the clues that he gives us as to how to live our spiritual life, in life, daily life also, very deeply. So, these are the things that I would say have struck me.

Finally, I had gotten [Baba's assignments to me] done ... This had been a very busy time from 1952 until the mid 50s when I was finishing that [*Listen, Humanity*] off, and again Dodd, Mead [the publisher] going to work on it. I had had my nose to the grindstone in so many airports, and strange hotels, for such a period of time that when that was done I just relaxed. And the next two or three times that I saw Baba I was just totally relaxed and having a helluva good time. Excuse me for putting it that way. And Naja's herb omelets. Oh my gosh, Oh.

Well, if you've never had an herb omelet to begin with, you know, you had better build that sanskara fast. Because it's worth it. And to have Naja, Baba's own personal cook do it, oh this was heaven. Every time I would arrive, Naja would come tripping out and say, "Now Don, would you like a herb omelet?" And well you know the answer, I didn't say, "Three or four of them," but I certainly said, "Yes!"

It was a wonderful time. So this went on, and I enjoyed myself thoroughly after all of the hum and hurrah and the mayhem of editing the first two books. And, you know, after Baba's gets done giving me a morning embrace, you all know what he would always ask me, "Did you sleep well? Did you eat well? Did you digest well? Did you have a good movement at the toilet?" and so on … and when I didn't, out came the orange drink {Baba's favorite laxative. Don laughs} Which produced immediate results always, I have never found its equal. And so we get through that …

Do you see how Baba takes care of you? Isn't it incredible? The first things, "How are you? What are you doing about your body?" And when I would see Baba receiving people that he hadn't seen in a long time, and see a guy who looks pulled down, and Baba would hold up the line for fifteen minutes to find out why. Why, you say. "Why?" And then Baba would get to some point in the person's health habits, and he would give instructions to that person, what he had to do, "Take care of your body. What good does it do to be spiritual if you lose your body and can't be spiritual at all?" These are the exact words I witnessed Baba to use for a young worker who looked almost like a skeleton. He would say it in words like that, I'm not being, uh ... joking! I heard Baba say that to this boy.

So, here we were and on about the third trip, Baba had gone through this roster of questions, and I had replied, and then he said, just out of the clean blue sky, "And Don, what are you doing about my words now?"

I thought I had finished his words. What more was I supposed to do? I didn't have anything, I said ... But, you know, actually I had a guilty conscience. I have to admit that. I see Laurent smiling at me, he knows. I was trying to gloss over something or another here but I couldn't quite do it because actually I think it hadn't been more than a month after I had gotten *Listen, Humanity* off to the printers and was relaxing when I suddenly said – God, this is too good to be true, this isn't going to last.

I've got a worker nature, too. I'm not a "shaker," but I am a "mover." So, I felt something probably had to be moved, and that I was goofing off and taking too much time doing it. I said to, uh ... my guilty conscience, "What do you mean?"

Baba said again, "Well, what have you been doing about my words?"

I thought – Now how am I going to side-track him? Because he's got another ... another project up his sleeve here some way or another – {Don laughs} I'm tired still, I want some more free time.

Then I thought up what I thought was the most beautiful reply, a lovely one, "Baba, I've just been enjoying your presence."

Hearing this, Baba gave me the big smile. {audience laughs lightly} I thought – Boy, that's great – and I relaxed and off we went onto another subject, and I thought I had neatly side stepped that one {Don laughs to himself} maybe to eternity, who knows? Not more than two or three more minutes, and

Baba suddenly cuts Eruch almost in mid-stream and says, "Don! But Baba means it. *What are you doing about my words?*"

I knew then that I hadn't slipped anything over on him at all, he was right on the track. I knew I had finally to face up, so I said, "Well, actually, there are all these young 'hippies' who are coming into the Sufi door and asking about Inayat Khan's poems, and things of this sort, and I've often thought that from what I remember of the *Discourses*, they probably should be the thing that they would really cotton onto."

Baba looks very interested, and wants to know about the hippies. I've taken so much time on other stories, I am not going to tell you about this first group of four hippies, but I can say that they were incredible. One day we'll sit and bat that one around. At any rate, I said to Baba, "I think they need the *Discourses*."

Although I had not read it in years at that time, I remembered rather well the Deshmukh edition. Deskmukh was a tremendously intelligent and careful worker, and he had a superb English vocabulary. "But," I said to Baba, "you know, there is one problem. I noticed in reading the *Discourses* that Deshmukh did, he uses typical, rather inverted, Indian sentence structure, and not English-American sentence structure. So unconsciously I quickly transpose things around and I suppose that probably decreases my efficiency ten, twenty, thirty per cent."

Then I had a bright idea, so I said, "Baba, you've got so many really wonderful workers in England and America who are expert scholars, why don't you get one of them to restyle the Deshmukh sentence structure?"

Baba looked at me with triumph, real triumph in his eyes, and what does he do? He says, *"You do it."*

So there we are. {laughter} Of course I kick myself all over the lot for patting myself prematurely on the back, and thinking I had evaded more work so expertly. But I did settle down to what Baba told me to do, and into this now enters another of the principal reasons I had to tell you about this. It's another of the central pillars of what we have got to remember that Baba tells us about his words.

I've already told you [in past group meetings] about all the discourses on meditation, and why this fact is terribly important because it involves not just the Path of Love, and other terribly important things such as Baba's Manifestation (even though I don't dare talk to any of the Mandali about it). But in addition to all that, when I was about two-thirds, three-quarters of the way through the editing [of *Discourses*], every time I would come for a visit, Baba would say, "Well, how are the *Discourses* coming?"

Finally it was evident that Baba was getting just a little impatient. Stevens has been running around on all these field trips, you know, and lovely hotels and wonderful dinners and not doing enough concentrating on Baba's *Discourses*. I could sort of feel this thought somewhere in the background.

Finally, on one occasion, Baba says very simply and directly, "Well, Don aren't you getting fairly close to putting the work in the hands of a publisher to print what you have finished?"

{Don coughs hard}

I said, "Well, yes Baba."

{as an aside about the coughing} As a matter of fact, Marion, it isn't ... Oh, sorry ... I thought she was getting me a glass of water, but this is a post-nasal drip, so it is a different kind of hoarseness. This is a post-nasal drip that drains into the lungs, so it's not in the part where the water does any good. {returning to the subject} So, as Baba asked me about a publisher ... *every time I remember this story, I remember my sense of what spontaneously I just had to say to Baba, and as I said it to him I was horrified, totally horrified at what I was saying.*

What I said to Baba was, "Yes, it is just about ready to go to the publisher, but I don't know what good it's all going to do."

Can you imagine saying that to the guy who gave them [the *Discourses*] out and had been using them for decades by that point? At that time, all during that time, it was his most important work and they were terrific. And I was saying to him that sprucing this up into a more acceptable edition was waste-time.

Obviously, as soon as I said it I thought – My God, the heavens are going to drop on my head now. – I looked quickly at Baba to see his reaction to these completely unpremeditated words. He did look a bit surprised, and then he leaned back in his chair. I remember it to this day, and my sense of horror 'cause boy I thought lightning was going to strike.

Looking surprisingly relaxed, Baba said, "What do you mean by that, Don?"

This was Eruch's translation of the gestures {audience laughing} but boy I could see what was really going on by the way he looked at me in the eyes. No escape. I knew I had to follow along. All this was back in the days (which are certainly not finished now) when people were talking about anything to do with intellect, logic, even philosophy as being an obstacle on the Path. The "in" words were that the Path was from the *heart* and *spontaneous*. All of these (intellect, logic, philosophy) are not only – not a help – but they cause a slowing down, and become an obstacle. I had been fed this from so many, many people. This was back in, especially, the hippie days, when it was all spontaneity and love. That was it. Anything to do with philosophy, or that was strung together in a pattern which made sense, which stuck together, was anti-spiritual. Just frankly, bluntly so.

I had begun to get rather discouraged with all of this. I had been [philosophically] fed, and had it tossed back at me. Usually people were polite when they did this because they knew that I'd been involved with *God Speaks* and with *Listen, Humanity*, so they would be polite about it, but still we got to know each other very, very deeply and frankly.

Now I have to tell you, just very simply, that I knew that their attitude was a major block in their own spiritual ongoing. There were so many beautiful, frank, honest, truly searching people around, it was astonishing. And so many of these kids [aged] 16, 18, 20, 22, 28, and so on, were some of the most wonderful, truly honestly beautifully searching people that I have ever been around in all my life, and they go on continuing their search. A lot of you are from that age.

You know, if you love somebody and you see that they are neglecting some important avenue, or have blocked off, blanked out, a whole important resource, it makes you sad. Then you wonder – how under the sun can I help them remove that particular obstacle? What they were saying had a certain import, a certain honesty, a certain factuality to it. I don't say to the contrary, but I knew how much I had gained from all of this work with Baba's words. By that time, for me, it was incredible to review the resources I had been given and the things that happened to me. I'd been around them now so much, and seen their effect on me. All this was what lay in back of my seemingly heartless comment to Baba.

So, when Baba said, *"What do you mean by that?"* I knew I had to be honest. I said, "Baba there are so many of some of the most wonderful seeking people that I have ever known in my life who regard any sort of words strung together in any sort of logical fashion as not only being not a help, but an actual detriment on the Spiritual Path."

Baba then stopped the conversation short by simply looking over at Eruch and starting to wiggle his fingers at him. The two of them had this conversation business down to a fine art because as Baba wiggles his fingers Eruch is replying in Gujarati, so here you have the perfect two-way conversation for both sides. It would carry on twice as fast that way and yet be understood perfectly. So it went very rapidly. After a few moments Baba looked back at me. This was one of those few times when I saw Baba look really hurt. He must have known this, and he did look hurt. I think this sort of attitude hurt him deeply, and he let me see it. But he simply said, *"And do they say this about Baba's words?"*

Now there was the real question, of course, and the one that disturbed me deeply, because it was Baba's own words that were on the chopping block for so many, many, many of these truly searching people.

So, I said, "Yes Baba." And then I knew that "yes" wasn't enough. Because there was a deeper aspect that had hurt me even more deeply than had these searching people, and that was that some of the most truly sincere, deeply loving people, of Baba himself, had said with almost pride, "I have never read a word that Baba has written."

I told Baba that, but I was very careful that he understood that in my estimation, the people who had said this, in many instances (not many-many, because not many people said that) included deeply sincere, very, very honest, very meticulously searching people totally devoted to Baba himself.

Then Baba went into another huddle with Eruch at the side. After about … it was a long time, maybe five or ten minutes … Baba motions to Eruch and Eruch says, "Don, Baba's been trying to explain something to me that is difficult to put into words – a concept – but the closest that I can get to it is that Baba says that when he gives out his words in the careful manner that I have explained to you twice about *God Speaks*, he gives the key essences of ideas to a Mandali, who writes it up and brings it back to Baba and he meticulously goes over it. *When Baba gives out his words in the manner that I have described to you, Baba attaches something to it,"* and he said, "this is where I can't get the meaning precisely, and Baba can't explain to me in enough detail to get the proper words, but the closest I can come to it is, *he attaches to each word something which is similar to an atomic bomb of spiritual energy."*

Then they let it stay there, and Baba and Eruch go back into "conversation" again for a few moments. Then Eruch comes back to me with another shorter statement, but very, very precisely said, *"And Baba wants you to understand that if a devotee works with his words, even though he may not understand two words intellectually, still enough of that atom bomb of spiritual energy will be absorbed by him automatically, to be of enormous importance in his own spiritual ongoing."*

Well, that was a helluva big important point that had been placed before me. Then still more, as Baba finished up, Baba gesticulating as Eruch said these words to me, as Baba pointed his finger at me, *"And it is your responsibility to explain to my devotees what Baba has explained to you today."*

Now you see why we are here on the fiftieth anniversary of Baba putting my nose to the grind-stone. This is one of the most important things, of course, that Baba has ever put into words for us. So, there we are with what came out of *Listen* ... not *Listen Humanity*, but the *Discourses*.

The *Discourses* were eventually republished in a little edition (three volumes by a Japanese printer). Good heavens, I think we paid something like twenty USA cents a volume, in those days, to have them printed in Japan. You know, we have to tell you some of these practical details while we're about it.

Things then went along quietly for a bit, but it wasn't for terribly long. You see, Baba doesn't let much time waste. I think we had just barely gotten out the little three volume blue Japanese edition of the *Discourses* when Baba said to me, "Well, now Don, you're over in Europe almost all the time now, what's your impression about what's going on in Europe?"

To fill you in on a bit of background, we had just gotten out these books in English, you see, when I was shifted over permanently in my petroleum work from America to Europe. I had been traveling a lot there, but my official point was now turned over to London. And Baba wants to know what I am finding out about young people there. That was back in the days when Delia [DeLeon] had just written me a special letter saying, "Don, a very interesting thing has happened. There were four, I think you call them 'hippies,' that knocked on our door at the [Meher Baba] Association meeting, and we invited them in. We really don't know what to talk to them about, and we know that you had been doing work with hippies in America, so is there any way that you could arrange to be at our next meeting? [Can you arrange your schedule] because they said they would like to come back and then you could meet them and see what happens."

I did as Delia requested, and went and met the four hippies. It was just exactly like history repeating itself. It was like the first four hippies that knocked on Murshida Duce's door to hear more about Inayat Khan's poetry, and Murshida Duce phones and says – Don, I don't know what to do with these guys ... – she didn't say guys, "these young people." And so that started off ... can you imagine, we did two years, three years of three month introductory courses in basic mysticism for those hippies?

Courses were in San Francisco with the original four hippies: Gary Gussik, another Gary, Doug Martin, and one other fellow, followed shortly by Bob Royeton.
—Don Stevens

To the first four in San Francisco I had said, "Well, you're asking questions that are so right, and so profound and so important, that we can't go about it in just the hit-and-miss fashion you're doing. The only thing I can suggest is that if you want to sit down one night a week, for three months, I'll try to bone up and do some homework and we'll talk about basic mysticism through the centuries, from as far back as we can trace it up through Meher Baba at present." It wasn't designed to be totally Meher Baba, just basic mysticism.

Of course I knew, and they eventually knew, that Baba was the apex, the current, great chapter in it. Those four kids came, but when they came to the first meeting, I think they were seven or eight, and that surprised me. And the next meeting it was fifteen, and the next meeting it was twenty-five. So I said, "Now look, we've got to have an understanding. The absolute limit for this group is thirty-five people. If more than that (any of your other friends want to come) we'll form a new group at the end of three months.

Three months later they finished and another group of thirty-five came. We did that for two, somewhere between two and three years. They were some of the most incredibly, beautifully exciting people I have ever been around in my life. And such exciting things happened to so many of them, as a matter of fact. So here's Baba saying to me, "Well, Don, what's going on in Europe?"

And here I am with all of that memory of what happened to all of the original hippies there [in San Francisco] and now, we suddenly get four hippies knocking on the Association and Delia feeling something should be done. So that was the point I was trying to get over [to Baba] about redoing the *Discourses*. "But," he said, "what about other countries?"

So here's another little chapter in what Baba, himself, laid out. He said, "Well, probably we should start thinking about doing some translating." And you know, they say you can never teach an old dog new tricks, well, this old dog never learned. So when he said about translating, I said, "Oh yes, yes."

First of all we talked about what languages they ought to be translated into, and Baba and I, pooling Baba's wisdom and my ignorance, decided that French, German and Spanish should be the three languages. I said, "Yes, I think that's great. I think your basic works should be translated into those languages, and I know you've got very competent people in each country who can translate them, Baba."

"You do it!" [Baba said to me]

Isn't he awful, Norah? Isn't he shocking? After all these years. What was this, ten-fifteen years later? I'm still just finishing off English editions of works agreed to between us, and then comes all this translating work. But hold on. And of course, I knew I had Baba this time.

I said, "Baba, I've done a lot of work in those three languages, because I do business there all of the time, but I can't possibly translate. It's too technical for me, Baba."

[Baba responded] "Well Don, of course you can't translate them, but you supervise them. You are responsible for them."

And that of course is where we were and, in fact, still are. But you know, the strange thing, the really, really remarkable thing is, when we get right down to it (this is not pride) but just to show you how he knows, and how he prepares ahead of time, each time when we would have a major book translated for the first time, then I would feel compelled myself to take the translation and compare it to the original English. Not only that, but by that time I had picked up enough specialized knowledge in these three languages in my business activities to know when the translator had missed Baba's sense.

Participant: Really?

Don: And do you know what that did? Baba has wheels within wheels, it's incredible. Remember what he told me? "If a devotee works with my words, he will automatically absorb an important part of the spiritual energy and this will be invaluable in his spiritual ongoing." So what do I do in carrying on the translation work I had agreed with Baba to supervise? I say – Well, OK, if you've gotta compare it word for word, all right, get on with it. If you've got more specialized knowledge esoterically in these words than a native French man has, for instance, you've got to do it and compare it – From the very start, each volume was done that way. The first one was into Spanish, the next one was into French, and then there was a small work in German, and so on. Then when we got into the French *God Speaks*, the Lemetais and I spent weekends, and weekends, and weekends, discussing and working and weighing the sense of words. I have never done such meticulous work with words in all my life. Then one day, when we got *God Speaks* published I sat back, and sort of took stock.

I could not believe the shift in major centers within myself that had gone on. And I had been totally unaware of them. I saw myself as Baba's guinea pig. I know this is true, that Baba didn't give us a little "pipe dream" about spiritual atom bombs. This is the truth. If you work with his words, even if you are not trying to put intellectual things together, some way or another, there is a spiritual osmosis that goes on, and you absorb the spiritual energy Baba attached.

I do not want to imply (come right back to you, Buster) I don't mean to imply that the logic of his words is unimportant. I do feel deeply that as an honest Baba lover we have got the mental capabilities to understand philosophically what he is saying, structuredly as well.

'Structuredly' is another Donism.

It is not just a question of trying to gulp up spiritual energy, but we owe it to the Avatar to try to be intelligent about what he is saying – the structure – because it's exciting. It is so personally tender, that's why I couldn't read that ["intuition from the kitchen front"].

You know, what you see in the structure of God's Creation is so tremendously reassuring and touching. Baba is quoted in *Lord Meher* as saying that, "*God Speaks* is not about love, but how to love God." And Eruch said about Baba's reassurances, in Mandali hall, "I worked on that, and I haven't seen any words in there that told me how to love God." But when I got done with the Lemetais the third time going over *God Speaks* I felt a tremendous love for God, with the way He had put creation together, and it made total sense to me. *When Baba says something, you know he's talking for real.*

Brendan, what were you saying?

Brendan: Lemetais, what's this?

Don: Lemétais is a family name, Françoise and Daniel.

Brendan: What I was going to say was the *God Speaks* which you are at pains to explain was set out by Baba letter by letter (or about) is not language specific. The bombs that are attached to these words.

Don: You know, this is a darn good point you raise, Brendan. To me, just simply, bluntly, the first time I ever got into a translation I had to say to myself honestly – Don, what happens to those atom bombs when it is translated into another language? And, I just had to say, when I got done with some of these translations and people started, for the first time, reading translations, I saw that things happened to them, inside, which were identical with what happened to people reading the original English. Some way or another the Avatar knows what he's doing and he takes it over, but we have to do a darn good faithful translation, in the sense of Baba's Sense. Now if I still haven't answered the question, push me further, Brendan.

Brendan: No that's fine, but you're adamant as to the limit of Baba's words. They don't extend through chapters nine and ten [of *God Speaks*] for example. And then you did a translation which has no input from Baba (if you put it like that) and yet that is Baba's words, and contains his spiritual atom bombs. I'm not sure that I am asking a question.

¶ Don: No, no, no, it's a good one. And I'm glad you asked 'cause it's a realistic question. I think that Laurent would like to pop in something there.

Laurent: I would, because I've been going over this "atom bombs" thing for quite a while now, and I don't know if Don agrees with me on this, but my feeling on the "Baba's words with the atom bombs" has to do with if it was Baba's idea, or his desire, that it be done. That then the words are charged. And the, "You translate this into these languages" [from Baba to Don] is part of the carrying of that charge. That's just my own feeling.

Norah: When you said the atomic energy is automatically transferred, and you absorb energy, well it doesn't say that it's anything to do with intuition, which one often thinks.

¶ Don: No, Norah. "Work, work," Baba says. {Norah interrupts}

Norah: Nothing to do with understanding.

¶ Don: Work. Nothing to do with understanding. He said, "… even if he does not intellectually understand two words…"

Norah: No, I mean, the transfer doesn't have anything to do with transferring understanding.

¶ Don: No, no.

Norah: And it's not to do with…

¶ Don: {Norah speaking at the same time as Don} You don't understand it, [it's with] spiritual energy.

Norah: intuition, which I'd been thinking that it was to do with.

¶ Don: Hmmm. Yeah. Not according to Baba.

Norah: No.

¶ Don: Brendan?

Brendan: On that basis, Don, why is it necessary to have the *God Speaks* for example, in anything other than English, if no understanding is required? A Spanish person can understand the Roman alphabet and…

❡ Don: You've got the answer to that. What Spanish person who doesn't understand English will take a book on faith and read it in English? Hmm? How nuts do you have to be, is all I can say.

{Don a little tense, lots of side talk and noise}

Renate Moritz: I do think that there are bad translations, and wrong translations. However, we have got a few good translations, so the bad translations will be detected, and things will have to change. Because, you know, the sentence structure and the thought structure are so complex. It's a huge work and task for any translator.

❡ Don: A Herculean task.

Renate: You know, the German *God Speaks* is finished now by a fantastic man in Germany.

❡ Don: And Renate is proofing that, by the way, an enormous task.

Renate: And reading, sometimes I translate, because it is so complex, the English sentence in my way and compare that to what he has translated because by just reading it I can't actually judge whether he is right, it is so extraordinary. I don't know whether you see that. These words are so complex, these sort of boxes of sentence blocks and this is (and I said this to David) I said, you know, there is so much knowledge behind this translation, I just doubted whether this has happened every time. But never mind about it, we seem to have some translations which are excellent, so there will be a comparison possible.

❡ Don: Brendan?

Brendan: Well, I was just going to suggest, since I think your criticism of my argument is unfair, Don.

❡ Don: Um-hmm …

Brendan: That if somebody wants to satisfy the machinations of their tortured mind (it's Chapter 10 [of *God Speaks*] there), they can read a translation, and if they want the spiritual atom bombs, they can read the English.

¶ Don: All I can say is it doesn't satisfy me Brendan.

Brendan: Well, I don't want to get into an argument.

Rosemary Harris: Don?

¶ Don: Yes, Rose.

Rose: Have they been done into Braille?

¶ Don: I don't know of any of Baba's books that have been done in Braille.

Norah: No, I was thinking it's a fairly vital field.

Participant: … wouldn't be a translation, it would just be the same, wouldn't it, only put in a different …

Rose: Yes, but I was thinking how important that must be.

¶ Don: I don't know anyone who has ever tackled that project.

Laurent: Are you going to tell [Rose] to do it?

¶ Don: I'm not Baba. {laughter and side talking}

Bruce Milburn: I think the thing is, though, that you may not understand necessarily what you read, but the effort to understand what you read is the important component within receiving, or undoing, or allowing the spiritual charge to jump across the gap. I mean, if you read without the effort, I don't think that necessarily unlocks it. I think there has to be a genuine attempt at reading it, with that in mind. It's not just reading for the sake of it, you know, one, two, three, four words, wallop-wallop. There's a bit more to it, and that small effort is a big difference.

¶ Don: Well, back to Stevens on that one because to me it was extremely noteworthy that in some fashion or another, as Baba discussed this, the word "work" came up several times. It was in the sense that you have got to put some sincere focused effort into it, some way or another. I have seen some people go rather to extremes of trying to find the way that effort on their part could be applied, especially to *God Speaks*, where let's say their immediate contact with the logic of the words could not rouse their interest to the point where they could put real continuing concentrated work into it, so they would have to find a new formula to express work. If this doesn't mean anything, I'm sorry, but there were two or three rather stunning examples of that that impressed me tremendously.

People have tried, for instance, reading it by themselves. They've tried reading it in groups. They've tried reading it in a small study group that tackles it this way, or that specialized way. I think one of the most beautiful examples of all was Norma Miles' beautiful letter, which we printed in *Neti Neti* and which will come out in the new little book on intuition in which she said, "Don, Keith got after me so much, and so long, and was so convinced of the importance of working with *God Speaks* that after trying this with a group and that with another little tiny circle of friends, and so on, I finally remembered that I am so tactile, and form conscious, that I wondered what would happen if I took a paragraph and wrote out the words long-hand." And you remember she said after that, "It was incredible, suddenly one day that paragraph came to life in a fashion that just put so many parts of my life in order, that had never been in order. And none of it related intellectually to the problems in my life, it wasn't that I suddenly understood it and how it applied to my life, but something or another vital was transferred. And that was the meaningful mode of transfer, when I myself wrote out the paragraphs," because that corresponded to her – what shall I say – *study-meaningfulness-style*.

Work is key. Work.

Laurent: Do you think then, Don, that it would be fair to say that it is not important how one works with Baba's words, as long as one does work with Baba's words? In other words...

Don: It has to be meaningful for something inside of you. It has to correspond to something that transfers back into your subconscious mind.

Norah: It seems to me these different ways of doing it, work together. I mean you can ... you've got a bit of *God Speaks*, and you're fairly familiar with it, so you've got a fair idea of what it's on about, but you can go back and read it and get something quite different out of it ... some insight that doesn't seem to follow from what you knew.

Don: Yes, I think that's still another thing, that there are let's say, hidden structures of meaning that are layered, and layered, and layered ...

Norah: Yes.

Don: OK, all right, this time you get to this layer, and you think – why didn't I see that six years ago? And then a year or two later, in that exact same thing, suddenly you see – Oh my gosh, there's all of this in back of that that's implied. So there's a layering of meaning. There's a great tradition in mystic literature, that truly great mystic writing is layered in this manner, and progressively you get to deeper and deeper [layers]. But that, I think, is different, because Baba said so very clearly and simply (I took him so terribly seriously), "even though two words do not make intellectual sense, you will still..." and so on and so on. But, he emphasized that you've got to work, and how? What is meaningful work for you? There is the key.

Richard Turner: Does that mean that the atom bomb charge has no effect on somebody who is not receptive to it? So that if you say, read it, you read *God Speaks* to someone who wasn't inclined to read it, or whatever ... it wouldn't have an effect on them?

Don: Richard, I am so naïve that I would say that even a person who has no interest in it, and for some reason or another just assigns themselves the grind of doing it, it will break through.

And to me, there is the great example from Baba himself when he talks about selfless service, which he says is one of the greatest things for disciplining, and getting the ego under control. He says that if you try to do some selfless service, you will likely be so terribly, terribly aware of the ego-centeredness of what is supposed to be selfless service that you are doing, that you may be honestly horrified and say – this is not for me – and be tempted to give it up. But Baba encourages one to persist in one's efforts at selfless service, as the final value is so great that you owe it to yourself to continue to strive, and to strive. Finally, because of its innate truth, the great value of such service will gradually pierce through to you and become real. That says so much to me.

I believe that you can have simply an intellectual conviction that something is good, or has got something for you, and when you try it for the first time you may say – Awful, my heavens, what a mess. – But then you decide to make another trial. OK, all right, go back, push, try, try again, keep trying, and just have some faith in the person who knew enough to say, "This has got real gold at the end of the rainbow here. So keep on."

So, you just say – I trust that guy, so I'm going to keep trying and see what the hell happens. – And I think virtue is finally rewarded. I'm an old fashioned romanticist there.

Keith Ashton: Don, maybe you can gauge it that the easier that it is for you to read, the closer you are getting to Baba, in terms of the veils maybe disappearing, the sanskaras lessening, and you can accept it more. After all, it's our journey from the Whim to God Realization, so [God Speaks] is about us anyway. And so we are recognizing our journey, our selves.

Don: You know, for some reason I don't connect easiness of perceiving the sense of it with one's progress on the Path. I'm not sure the two things are linked, Keith, but anyway...

Keith: It just occurred to me that, maybe, because I find it very difficult to read (I've read probably a quarter of it) so it just struck me that maybe that's the reason, because, you know, the worldly sanskaras are in the way, sort of blocking me.

¶ Don: I doubt it, knowing you, I just doubt that. I think you're an awful lot farther along than you give yourself credit for, and I'm not trying to butter you up.

Female Participant: I don't think … I don't agree with you Keith, because … maybe it's more something that should speak to your heart, instead.

Keith: Yes, Baba did say that, didn't he, that it was for the intellect, in the future that people would come to Baba through their intellect, initially?

¶ Don: I don't remember that…

Participant: Where is that, Keith?

¶ Don: I just don't know.

David Lee: I'm just wondering whether sometimes we can actually be looking at life in a different way, without realizing that we're looking at life in a different way. It starts to resonate in a process, but the point at which it begins you might not always be aware that it has started to shift. Do you see what I mean?

¶ Don: Strange things do go on totally without your realizing that anything is happening, until one day suddenly it bursts through and you say, "Good heavens, all of this has been going on inside of me and I wasn't even aware of it." So give that sort of thing a little bit of a chance also. The fact that you can work & see no results from it doesn't mean that there are not deep results inside of yourself. This I have found out again & again & again.

Participant: I must say, Don, that (picking up on David) would resonate. When I read the evolution from gas form to stone form, that was very profound. There was no doubt about it. I mean, something happened. And the strange thing is that I haven't really gone back to *God Speaks,* but it was very profound for me, the experience of it.

Wayne Smith: Don, also part of the work is working with companions: *inner-links.* It's also very important in how we, kind of, work with Baba's words.

❧ Don: Yes. I think that's an awfully good point. Why don't you carry that on a bit further, Wayne?

Wayne: Personally, in my own life, it has been easier to work with Baba's words when I've been working with other people, and we've been reflecting and thinking about things together. And I think, more and more so, that's the case. I think part of the whole work is with other people, and there's something very important that happens with the spiritual charge of Baba's words to do with inner-links as well.

John: All I can say is that, I've approached *God Speaks* in a variety of different ways, but especially the end of the reincarnation chapter in which Baba raises along the line that obviously sanskaras have to be experienced while we're in the physical body.

❧ Don: He sure does say that, doesn't he?

John: And I wish I'd done some Wayne-Smith-type-work, which I have still to do, because just dipping in arbitrarily a couple of days ago into volume one of the (old three volume) *Discourses* … There is a grand theme here, that opposite sanskaras have to be experienced while we're in the physical body. I find it difficult working in isolation, not difficult, practically impossible, but that's something that I would appreciate, to work with you, Wayne. That has altered my whole attitude, not only towards life, which is one thing, but the whole of life. What Baba says has an enormous impact, because that's as great as anything that is in Tolstoy's *War and Peace,* or Dosteyevsky, or in Shakespeare. That is a grand theme of world literature, opposite sanskaras have to be experienced while we're in the physical body.

I think that is tremendously exhilarating, but I do need to work on that with other companions, to see where, with the inner-links, where it would actually lead. Maybe there's something in me that's a little bit frightened of where it may lead.

¶ Don: I think Norah wants to add on to that.

Norah {to John}: You say, "Sanskaras have to be experienced in the *physical body*," but you can put the intonation different-ly. You can say, "*Sanskaras* have to be experienced in a physical body." Do you see what I mean? Not only that if you've got san-skaras that they've got to be experienced in the body, but that is something that you have to do in the body, it's one of the tasks.

John: It 'tis. You can't sort of … Baba is not fooling around here. Baba is for real. I mean, this has a very slow, you know, drip, drip, drip effect, because, I think, you know, my ego finds … still finds this very threatening. In one way I rejoice at it, in another way I'm appalled at it.

¶ Don: Well, the ego resists getting killed off. {lots of back-ground conversation and noise}

Bruce {To a female participant}: I've just had a sense that your question, sorry I don't know your name …

¶ Don: Kavita.

Bruce: Your question wasn't really answered. I mean in the sense that, I may be wrong, but I felt that you thought that be-cause it's seemingly partially an intellectual process, it needed a bit of reading *God Speaks*, which I think is true. I think what I'm saying is that we all have different orientations of how we go. A bit like water, we take the least line of resistance, and some things, you know, like *God Speaks*, is for many very difficult to read. Now I'm just going back to my own case. I don't have an intellectual bent, but many years ago I persisted, I think through encouragement from one or two other people. And I was sur-prised to find that somehow through reading [*God Speaks*] some emotional content was unlocked. I was really surprised, because I find reading that sort of material impossible. But somehow, my companions (one or two individuals) gave me the encouragement to give it a try, and I did persist. Once or twice, or maybe a few more times, and I was truly surprised to find how it did unlock something which I had thought would be impossible. I would just pass that on to anyone, that when you look at it you think – My God, what the hell is going on? – But then …

Wayne: I suppose part of it as well is that when you're engaged in working on Baba's words you're actually focused on Baba. And maybe that's the most important thing, you know?

Don: Why not?

Wayne: Yeah. And that's what it's all about.

Don: Marion?

Marion: Well, it does seem to me that this might be the very link. The head is what reasons you to get the book, and you approach it with the head to read these words, and those words unlock the heart, and you get the *balance of the head and the heart*, and that is where this wash of energy comes in – when you get it from the page. It's so incredible. It's your head … head is going to make you do it …

Laurent: Heart is going to get you through it.

Male Participant: Well, on another note there, on a practical note, if you get through a very difficult task in life, which you didn't want to do probably in your mind in the first place, and you do it, there is the release of getting on with the rest of life. {various background comments are made}

Renate: {starts out difficult to hear her} … it's like in our jobs. When we bring our children along it becomes difficult. But I feel once we see that this area also, is as much a real area, we learn gradually to make that effort. We have to get accustomed to it. I think always when you start to have a child you think – Oh

My God, this is just too much – and then you get into it. And in the end you don't know how many [separate] efforts you spend every day on this, and you know this is part of us, it's part of us.

Male Participant: But a job done like Don finished, where he had a month off before the next one, actually meant that he could open up, loosen up and enjoy himself, but then he had to get back, {a loud clap is made} to the next stage.

⁋ Don: Interesting to reflect back after 50 years. Anyway, it was pretty well outlined by the Boss-man himself, that's very obvious.

Kavita: {hard to hear her} Baba … not much that's clear in our lives …

⁋ Don: No, it's certainly true, Kavita, that there have been very few moments practically in my life that have not been dictated by orders from Baba, or the wishes of Baba. That's the way it has worked out.

David: Norah was talking before the lunch break about this interaction between the head and the heart that can … it's not always very clear, and you know, you think – this is my head working now, and now this is my heart working – There is subtle interaction going on all the time, and so what you were saying, Marion, about having an intellectual motivation to pick up *God Speaks*, I'm not quite so sure. I think somewhere in that, there's a heart-thing that's going on in there. It is constantly "to-ing and fro-ing," really.

⁋ Don: Well, did we sort of exhaust that subject? {laughter from audience} A bit of back and forth.

John: No, we still haven't talked about experiments. Another experiment is to read *God Speaks* out loud.

⁋ Don: That was one that Norma tried. She tried several before the hand-written one.

John: This is a fascinating talk which could go on all night, but there is a problem of assimilating, doing a good job, assimilating, digesting Baba's words in *God Speaks* with one's mind, with one's heart, with one's gut feelings as well. It's a major job, whichever way we approach it.

Norith (Docherty): Can't we leave the assimilation to Baba and just do what he asked?

¶ Don: I'm not sure that satisfies the work principle. It seems to me that, you know, when Baba says "work," it's right up to the last stage of it, Norith. Maybe it's the way I'm built.

Norith: OK, I've read it, but I didn't know what I have taken in, and it hindered the assimilation for me. {aside thoughtfully} I meant that in a different way. I did read it, I didn't really want to but I did. But I don't know about the assimilation, that is what I meant, I left that to Baba. {everyone speaking at once}

¶ Don: But I wonder if it is assimilation that Baba is emphasizing. It's not so much assimilation I would look for, but let's say a new dimension unexpectedly opening somewhere in your inner life that I would take as being what *God Speaks*, and working on it, would do. Because that I've seen so many times, and people have always said, "Good heavens, I never expected it, but it happened out there, and I know the two things were connected, but how they were connected, I don't know."

Participant: Going back to my analogy I used just now ...

¶ Don: Go ahead.

Participant: I'd like to clarify it a little bit, because when you see a book, a book is pure intellect, how it got there, onto a page, printing, all the intelligence and knowledge has gone into putting it there. It came live from Baba, and was condensed into this intellectual form of how do you print, how does someone put it onto a page, all that computerization, etc. But the words, which came from Keith: "how does a stone become worm," to me that's *heart*, so you're bringing those two forms together at that moment. You've got to get the book – it's there, in a stored form, by the intelligence which has put it there. When the *mind* gets on to that, the *heart* can open when it sees these things are known to the heart, that the stone has become the worm, or the stone has become the plant, or the plant has become the worm. {laughing to herself} But those things are known to the heart.

Don: The stone goes on to metal. {everyone laughs}

Participant: OK. These things are known to your *heart*. Everything is stored in the heart. And the heart is supposed to be everything.

Don: You're going to get a few rebuttals on that one.

Participant: So that's why I just feel it connects with that deep knowledge that you've got within you. That's why I think the two there become the one.

Don: I think Keith is about to explode behind you. {laughter}

Keith: Well, I'm just interested in that rebuttal thing.

Don: Yes, that everything is stored in the heart, I thought that would produce a few explosions with a few people.

Norith: Can I read one sentence?

Don: Please, Norith.

Norith: It's about mind and heart, that was written in the 30s. *"When the mind encroaches upon the presence of the heart, it requires the assurance of conviction before it will sanction the release of love."*

Quote is from, *Silent Teachings of Meher Baba: Discourses and Conversations* (2001: New Jersey), compiled and edited by Naosherwan Anzar, Beloved Archives Inc.

Don: That's a pretty widely roving statement isn't it?

Participant: Let's hear that again.

Norith: Well, it is just a little bit I grabbed out, "When the mind encroaches upon the presence of the heart, it requires the assurance of conviction before it will sanction the release of love." So there's a … the conviction that will then … can release.

Participant: It's also worth remembering, something I first

heard from Adi Sr. [Adi K. Irani] who said that, "*The intellect has great difficulty in embracing contradictions. That it can do it, but not without a touch of suffering.*" And of course, suffering is the heart content.

Norah: Very interesting.

Laurent: {laughs} You've got Norah going. {background conversation}

Bruce: At the end of the day, [with head and heart] one always tries to dominate the other. One tries to be superior to the other, and we identify with that. The problem is that the two, as is so clearly brought out in the discourse on love, have to be brought into harmony with one another. But this is the thing that many of us refuse to do because we have a bent towards either the intellect or the heart, and it is so difficult to bring the two into equal … what? Equal power, equal whatever.

Participant: Balance

Bruce: Balance.

Renate: I would like to say that, you know, very often you would like to have the two tools, but sometimes *the heart isn't even open*, so one has to work on all ends really, constantly. Something like this, you know this book [*God Speaks*], gosh it is really a huge structure, and one can only say – but I will work on it. That's all that counts.

Don: Can I put in a word for somebody else? This is not for Don Stevens, but for Tom Hickey. I don't think many people here know Tom. He's a great Baba lover, and just retired university professor in philosophy and religion that really knows his stuff. He's gotten very deeply involved in a lot of e-mail exchanges, and one of the things he brought up at one point (when we were discussing the agenda for this weekend) was the fact that one should almost certainly realize that the balance between the head and the heart, even in a highly developed and well balanced individual, is not always necessarily the same. That in one circumstance, it will probably be more the head that is dealing with it, and in another circumstance more the heart. In other words, it doesn't have to be an exact fifty-fifty [50/50] in order to be valid. And I think this is a beautiful point he brought up.

Laurent: Just speaking to Renate, I know [Don] wants to get on with [his] agenda … but couldn't one also have a tiny-heart and a tiny-mind and bring them into balance? It's not the size that matters? {laughter in the audience}

❧ Don: I think this is inevitable isn't it? We're human beings, and some of us are tiny, and some of us are big lugs.

Participant: A perfect balance brings *Perfect Master* doesn't it? I mean that's the qualities of a Perfect Master. So, you're unlikely to have achieved this state.

❧ Don: Baba never said I was a Perfect Master at all.

> What Baba said was, "Don has an almost perfect balance of head and heart." —Laurent

Marion: Whose heart is it? Whose heart is it? Is it our heart? Or *Universal Heart*?

Participant: Heart in the Ayurvedic tradition is the "Chita" and it contains every single thing, and it is the mirror of the soul, but the soul can't move or know itself.

> The literal meaning of the word "Chita" is not easy to find. It has also been defined as "Mind Substance" by some. In the Glossary of *God Speaks*, "chit" is defined as: Divine Knowledge. —Laurent

❧ Don: Can I take the floor now? I am going to exercise the often unpopular arbitrary position of making a decision for the group, and that is that we are in a subject that is fascinating and has no end of things that one loves to reflect on and exchange, but we do have one, or two, or three, or four, or ten, or fifteen more items that we promised – I promised ourselves – we would get through.

I wanted to finish off, just a little bit more, in talking about assignments that I took on at Baba's request, because I am talking first of all about the history of Baba's words, that I know from Baba himself. Now just to finish off that background, because I've told you already about the major assignments and the *tremendously revealing comments that he made* at various stages of those assignments, that refer to the spiritual life that we're in. And he touched on, as if in passing, so many things that are so very pertinent to how we go about that life.

That part I've largely done, but I'll just finish off one other little corner before I take up one more very key topic, and that is *the resources available to us after Baba leaves the body.* What I want to do now for a moment is to describe several assignments that were given to me. These are in addition to the things that Baba himself, while he was in the body, talked over, gave me directions on, largely at least supervised the beginning manner in which they were carried on, and in some cases carried right straight through supervising until the very end.

Since Baba dropped the body, the [Avatar Meher Baba] Trust [in India] has asked me to do a number of other things for them, probably the most important being to supervise the granting of translation rights (anywhere in the world) for their copyrighted material, in any language, except within India.

That has also been an enormous amount of work. I would never, never possibly have been able to do even a small amount of it, either energy-wise or finance-wise if it had not been for Magestic Foundation, of which several of you are participants and have done an enormous amount of work in helping out. Also, I have to call to your attention a person whom you all know, and you always think of him as being a delightful character, and a real character, by the name of Claude Longuet. If Claude Longuet had not manually hauled and man handled so many, many projects, it would never have gotten done. Also, I just have to tell you that the original inspiration for the resources that have largely supported [Magestic] came at least eighty or ninety percent from Claude Longuet. Even though you rarely see him at a meeting, I think that one cannot discuss Baba's words, and assignments that Baba gave, without honestly bringing in the name of Claude Longuet, who never sits around waiting for praise. So, there we are.

Those, then, are the resources, assignments and projects, as well as some of the interesting and terribly central things that come up during the course of working out their trajectory. Now, I think we just have to get into the resources that are available after Baba has dropped his body, and I've listed here three major categories that we should at least try to start today (maybe we'll have to carry them over to tomorrow). I've found that it's a rare seminar for which we make an outline, and then get through much more than half of it. But we should at least do our damnedest to try as best as we can. So, I've listed these three resources, and I think we've got to take a really honest look at each of them:

1. *Unpublished manuscripts.* They turn up and people get very excited about them, and what is their true value? What is it?

2. Secondly, *diaries kept by Mandali and other close ones.* Resource material. I think probably the major use of those so far has been in Bhau's *Lord Meher.* And we have a big problem with attribution there, because Bhau did not attribute, and so we don't know what came from Chanji, and what came from Ghani, and what came from Dr. Donkin, and so on. At any rate, that's number two.

3. And then thirdly (now this has got to go in): *Appearances of Baba to close mandali and others close to him* during his lifetime.

Now, we've got thirty minutes. Yes, Laurent?

Laurent: Can you add to that last one also, appearances of Baba to people *after his physical lifetime*?

Don: I thought that's what three was about?

Laurent: You said, "during his lifetime."

❦ Don: "Close to him during his lifetime." People who were close to him.

Laurent: Oh.

❦ Don: Those are the ones that people tend to think would be the most valuable. If you had original contact with Baba, and then go on having apparently psychic visions of him now, most people would think that's more credible than someone who was born twenty years after Baba dropped the body, and has visions now of Baba. Maybe they are headings, "(a) and (b)" Appearances.

Participant: What was number three again, Don?

❦ Don: All right, I put it down as, "Appearances of Baba to close Mandali and others close to him during his lifetime."

{background discussion}

❦ Don: … That these people knew him during Baba's lifetime and now after Baba lifetime have visions of Baba.

John: {something about a psychic book}

❦ Don: Which psychic book?

Participant: Nan Umrigar.

❦ Don: Oh. Well, Nan never … well, it was her son, who ended up, after he was killed in the horseback accident, who was being taken care of by some gentleman (he'd never heard of the fellow) and eventually asked him who he was, and the man said, "I am called Meher Baba."

Norah: But you're thinking more of experiences, or visions, or voices from Baba not from …

❦ Don: I am talking about direct visions and voices from Baba, such as I felt in those three instances in my own experience. I could not associate them with anything but Baba's own words.

Laurent: So you're guilty also?

❦ Don: Oh yes, I'm right in the middle of the heap. Three times this happened to me in, what is it now, forty years, thirty years?

Participant: {can't hear the distant voice}

❡ Don: {even Don couldn't hear her}

Laurent {To Don}: "Nan did write to her …" she's saying.

Female Participant: But Nan said, Baba did write to her.

This is a complicated story. For more information see the book, *Sounds of Silence*, by Nan Umrigar

❡ Don: Oh, did she? I didn't see that as a matter of fact.

David: Don, what … where would you place the dreams that one can have where Baba appears in the dream, and they can be very powerful. I remember Kitty [Davy] saying once, that when one has a dream it can almost be like a vision.

❡ Don: Mm-hmm. Well, I wouldn't care whether we use the word vision or dream, or vision and dreams, you know. They're all the same general category. Norah?

Norah: Yes, I've had dreams where Baba actually speaks, you see, but I give them the greatest doubt.

Marion: Baba did say something on that, I can't quote the exact quote but I understood that Baba said – when I am in your dream it is real, it is real experience.

❡ Don: I haven't read that, Marion.

Marion: The twins. The twin brothers [Sohrab and Rustom Irani, Baba's twin nephews] … the fiancée of one of them had a vision of Baba (and the other twin was devastated because he wanted to get married, too) … and then the other engaged girl had the same vision exactly of Baba coming and blessing her. And around that …

❡ Don: Irrefutable.

Marion: I know Delia always told me, that if Baba was in your dream … discard any other dreams, but if Baba was in the dream then it was a dream to be taken seriously.

❡ Don: Well, there's a lot of rules of the thumb.

Norah: {hard to hear how she starts} … one's own wishes for some communication, wishful thinking, & all this comes into it.

¶ Don: Could I be a whip cracker again, and suggest we go back to point one, which is when Mani [Baba's sister] passed on, and manuscripts were found that were quite exciting ... But I think eventually we have to boil that down to, well, what are they? What is their value? And particularly, what is their value in relation to things that were put out by Baba, and published during his lifetime, directly from him? I think the most important there are the hand-scripts that are done in Baba's hand, obviously, and which are published under the title, *In God's Hand*.

What is that in relation to, for instance, the *Discourses,* as it is similar to the *Discourses* material? How do you handle the situation, for instance, where there is a difference in terminology about natural, non-natural and un-natural sanskaras? This is a typical example, which has come up several times, and some people regard them, I think Bhau himself regards them, (non-natural and un-natural) as being two totally different types of sanskaras.

You know, Baba himself during his lifetime gave us several definitions, I think there were four. Then, if we have not only non-natural but un-natural also, then that's still another one, and exactly where does it fit in?

That is one thing, and then there was a much longer, I think type-written manuscript, which it was felt by the Trust to be also from Baba, probably in the Prem Ashram days, which they feel Baba intended for use there. This is being worked on very carefully and will be published. But where does this take its place in Baba literature? This is an example of the important questions that inevitably arise and require the most careful handling, and I suppose there are very likely to be others found here and there. You know, life is still pretty young, as Baba hasn't been gone physically that many years.

Let's take an actual example, and dust it off and do a little bit of head scratching into the significance. *In God's Hand* was certainly written by Baba. I haven't perused it thoroughly, but in comparing it with original discourse material from the Deshmukh edition, which was put out in Baba's time and worked over by me and then others, it is different in its depth and also in the manner in which it is put. I think people felt that Baba wrote [*In God's Hand*] in a somewhat different style to appeal more to young kids, such as in the Prem Ashram. I think that's why they assumed that it was intended for the Prem Ashram. Then let's ask ourselves, how does this stack up in authoritativeness, dependability, and importance in relation to the *Discourses* themselves?

The chief thing that has come to my attention, so far, is this question about sanskaras, non-natural and un-natural, with the majority of people feeling that Baba used one [term] early in the game and decided against it, and later in life used the other [term]. In other words, un-natural was discarded and non-natural was used in his later life.

But the principal thing is that we shouldn't get confused and think here's still another form of sanskaras.

¶ Don: Laurent?

Laurent: Yes. I did read *In God's Hand* over and over again, over seven times, and nowhere did Baba use un-natural [in connection with the word sanskaras], he always said non-natural [in all his published literature]. And I also looked in all the other literature, and I never found Baba (in print) using un-natural [in connection with the word sanskaras]. Apparently Bhau likes that term, and he uses it. He uses it, but I've never seen Baba use it.

Baba does use the phrases "unnatural light" and "unnatural darkness" in the book *In God's Hand*, but he never says, "unnatural sanskaras."

¶ Don: But then it is in the printed thing [a longer manuscript found near the same time as *In God's Hand*] that is felt also to have been aimed at the Prem Ashram. They feel this too is Baba's. Is that then where the word un-natural comes from in connection with sanskaras?

Laurent: Is it published?

❡ Don: Well, I understand that Meherwan Jessawalla [Eruch's brother] and Ward Parks have been working like fury on editing it to get it ready for publishing. So, I am just saying, what do we have? What did Baba intend? What is the reputability [of the two newer documents]?

Participant: What's the suggestion, that Baba typed this manuscript?

❡ Don: No, he always had people typing for him, he had some obedient slaves around. Mani did an enormous amount of typing for Baba, and other people did also.

Bruce: Well, it's difficult to say, because you could look at the track record from how you described today, the manner in which it would seem key works were given out by Baba, in the sense he is very meticulous in the manner in which it has been given. But you know, things found later ... I remember looking at *In God's Hand* several times and thinking it was a work-up, or notes, for something that was a later completed work. It may well have been aimed at the Prem Ashram, but I never felt it was a final draft. But I have no conviction, pure conviction...

❡ Don: Does it matter whether it was a final draft? Suppose that it was a final draft, then what do you suppose happened to it, and what does that imply in relation to Baba's judgment of its value? Do you feel like answering that, Bruce?

Bruce: I don't think I understand your question. Sorry, Don.

Participant {To Don}: Without the specific say so from Baba, "Publish this ..." then it carries less weight, is that what you are saying?

❡ Don: Well, this is a question that I pose to the group here.

Wayne: ... the audience of these early manuscripts, I mean if they are meant for the Prem Ashram, obviously the boys there would have been of a certain age. Then in both these manuscripts, *In God's Hand* and the one that's being worked on, you know Baba might have used terminology that would have been more appropriate [for that age group]. Perhaps he thought the word "un-natural" would be better understood than nonnatural.

Male Participant: All right, we're making good points here, because this was Baba as the teacher before he, if you like, began to *awaken*. Nothing else was done for thirty years. So, it's a record, at that point, this is what was actually happening. It was the early stages, if you like, as a *teacher*. And then there's nothing for thirty years. So the thirty years surely has to be more important than anything that happened in the 20s.

Don: Laurent? Laurent, would you go ahead?

Laurent: I'm just going to say something simple, that may just *not make any sense*. But from my simple feeling about it, if Baba wrote it by his own hand, it's published. It's already down, it doesn't need to be in a book form, or distributed, it's already published. And maybe he just felt like that was all it needed right then.

Don: Well, I'm not arguing about whether it should be published or not, because I think most people feel that anything that comes directly from Baba should be available in print, but in, let's say, the evaluation of the work, its probable value. Is something that was not published (that was available but not published during Baba's lifetime), should that be evaluated as equally authoritative, and valuable, from Baba's philosophy standpoint, as another work that was published by him during his lifetime? To me, this is a fairly critical point.

Participant: I think – yes – because we don't know Baba's timing and when he wants us to ... {someone in the audience makes much noise}

¶ Don: Well, to that, as we've been discussing here, I've been thinking over my own observations of Baba's handling of material that he gave out. He knew and cared for it meticulously, he knew what he had done, where it was, and he was not a person to forget. So, the chances that he forgot a hand written manuscript (or a typed up manuscript) and is now saying [up in heaven], "Oh Glory Be, I forgot to do ..." so and so, "... we'd better get it out because it is an important part of the record." To me those chances are nil. To me, both of those manuscripts were deliberately abandoned by Baba because later, more – what shall I say? – more carefully worked out, or more mature things came along and so he simply abandoned them.

This is certainly what happened with his notes to Ghani [which became the supplement to *God Speaks*]. Baba was ready to junk it totally. And the fact that it wasn't junked can be a considerable point of confusion in the future. Because there are an awful lot of people who feel that even if he said he was ready to junk it, the fact is that it didn't get junked and that must have meant that he didn't want it junked, and really wanted Murshida Duce to accept it, and put it out. Frankly, there are an awful lot of people who insist that the supplement [to *God Speaks*] has equal spiritual authority to Baba's direct eight chapters. This, of course, I just can't buy. But some awfully good, intelligent people feel that way.

Wayne: Were Ghani's notes written by Ghani? I mean, what you've got are notes given to Ghani, written by Ghani.

¶ Don: All I can say is that Baba himself said, "When he [Ghani] died, I had one of the Mandali go to his room and take the notes that he had written up, which should have contained certain things I gave him, but in fact contained almost nothing of what I had given him." So, the pages were written by Ghani, and among his personal possessions.

Wayne: But then the notes that were discovered, written by Baba, people might argue these are … by Baba …

¶ Don: Oh, sure, I'm not saying that Baba's unpublished material is worth no more than Ghani. To me anything from Baba, whether published or unpublished, is damn valuable. But I would not give [Baba's unpublished material] equal priority with what he carefully got out and published, carefully handled by him, himself, during his lifetime. I would just say – No, no way – I just can't accept it that way. Baba was meticulous about what he did, and those things, he knew where things were, they didn't get, "lost and forgotten."

Don {To a woman}: Yes, you were just about to say something.

Female Participant: I was going to say I think they are valuable for what they are. I suppose like an artist, or something, has sketches and works stuff out and then does the sort of masterpiece from that. The sketches, in the future, are interesting to explain the masterpiece, and they …

¶ Don: They demand a good price, don't they?

Participant: Yes. {laughter and background comments}

John: Where does something like this new book on Mehera fall into this? It was apparently a long-awaited book that is about to come out. Where does this … How do we assess this?

¶ Don: I thank the lucky stars that David Fenster took all that research work and put it together. But I certainly don't equate that with *God Speaks* or the *Discourses*, or something like that. And I don't know whom David Fenster quotes. If he annotates and attributes properly, then it will have considerable importance. If, for instance, he's taken large parts from Donkin and Chanji, they would be the most authoritative sources that can be quoted. I would put people like that in category two just under Baba himself.

So, where David got his material is terribly important, and I hope to hell he attributed it well, as a good orderly book of that sort should be. I think we have got to be a lot more professional in this area in the future.

John: But how would you go about ... There's a major job with Bhau's [*Lord Meher*] ...

Don: This will be a huge job.

John: This is an incredibly large job, with *Lord Meher*.

Don: Well, can I just quickly tell you the history of that? When I went through *Lord Meher* early, I was surprised to see that nothing was attributed, and I knew that large segments had to be taken from the diaries of different people. I knew some of those people well enough to know that I, at least, would evaluate one Mandali's contribution much more than another. But in any case, it should be attributed to the proper Mandali. And so, I took this up with Bhau [Kalchuri], and Bhau simply said, "Well, this is Meheru's job, so why don't you talk to her?"

I wrote Meheru a lengthy letter, and Meheru thanked me and said, "I've taken it up with the Archives Committee, they have voted that this is a top priority, *the top priority project*, to attribute *Lord Meher*. Meheru then took it up with Bhau, and Bhau agreed that this was a top priority project, and that, as he found time, he would do the attribution. I wrote to Bhau saying, "Bhau, let's be just honest with each other. You're not terribly young, and you're not in terribly good health. If something should happen to you before," excuse me, this is the way I work, but I said, "If something should happen to you before you are able to do it, would you allow then David Fenster complete free reign to do the attributing? Because he worked with you for a long time. And would you mind, if you agree, if I talk to David so he knows he's the next in line in the spot."

I'm not the Archives Committee, but I felt this was so important. I did so much work on Baba's own direct words I felt this was the least I had to do in the circumstance. So Bhau said, "Absolutely." And I talked to David Fenster, and David said, "Well, I did a lot of work and I've got stacks of notes like that, and so that can be brought into it. But of course, Bhau is the principal one."

So then I wrote to Bhau, and said, "Bhau, you've had a terrible illness and things are not getting any less complicated, is it about time to get David Fenster into the act?"

Bhau wrote back and said, "I am just absolutely overworked, and I don't have any time to do anything of that sort. Take it up with Meheru again."

David Fenster then chipped in and said, "I am so busy with the Mehera biography, there's nothing I can do until I get done with that." So everybody is alerted as far as it can go for the present. I think it is well realized that this is a major, major work of major importance.

John: {inaudible comment}

❧ Don: Yes. But this is only one of several things. If you heard all the stories … Let me give you just one more example of the confusion that goes on here. Sometimes, I just get boggled by it. You know I am just being honest, and trotting out what I know, because this is rapidly coming to a focus now, Baba's words now, and what their importance is for the future, and it's damn big.

One of the things that has absolutely, completely befuddled me are the various different ideas and theories on who wrote what part of the *Everything and the Nothing*. One person says, "Well obviously it is Baba." Eruch told me, *"Well, Don, you got that all wrong. It is not Baba. Francis Brabazon was surreptitiously taking notes when Baba was talking*

Not to be confused with the book written by Bhau Kalchuri with a similar title, *The Nothing and the Everything.* —Laurent

to this businessman from Delhi. And this businessman from Delhi, nobod
knows why Baba ever spent so much time so happily with that man, and le
him ask questions by the yard, and so gradually over several visits when th
man came down, all this terribly important exciting material came out."

Eruch went on to say, "So Francis, when the visits finally stoppe
asked Baba for permission to write up the notes he had taken. I mear
he was a little bit afraid because he wasn't even supposed to be takin
notes."

This was Eruch's story to me. And so I said – Boy this sure puts
different cast on the whole thing. So, the *Everything and the Nothin*
with "Meher Baba" at the bottom [as the author], this is Francis Bra
bazon's polite way of saying, "Well, it isn't me, I was just the secretar
for the work." But he did a lot more than secretarying
he was the guy who took the notes, wrote up the note
and got it published. And both Mehera and Mani said that, next to th
Discourses, this is the book they love. I think it's an extraordinarily im
portant and beautifully written book, but this story is not particularl
well known. And I must add that two or three of the people who kno
the background well say, "But after that, Baba did a lot of work on it.
Well, did he or didn't he? I'm virtually certain Baba did just tha
How much work did he do? I want to get back to Bal Natu, an
one or two people, and find out really, does anybody really know ho
much Baba then put his hands into Francis' notes? I think this i
important. The *Everything and the Nothing* I think is a superbly goo
and important book. Besides, I think Francis is one of our greates
writers in the tribe. Can I talk any more frankly than that?

Mary Turner: Was it published initially during Baba's lifetime?

Don: Initially published in Australia.

Mary: When Baba was alive?

Don: Uhh, I can't remember that, Mary. I looked it up once an
I've forgotten just now. I think it was published after, but I'm … I'r
almost certain that Baba knew the manuscript and was pleased wit

Secretarying is a Donism.

the manuscript, from what I know.

Laurent: I almost don't want to say this but, I know a little bit about *Lord Meher* which I have to add a couple of layers to what you said, Don.

Don: Yes.

Laurent: My understanding is that *Lord Meher* was written in Hindi …

Don: Hmm.

Laurent: Translated into English by Feram Workingboxwalla.

Don: True.

Laurent: Typed up by David Fenster …

Don: True.

Laurent: And then I saw the difference (because of work I was doing) between what was typed up by David Fenster, and what got published. There are differences there because Hermes [Lawrence Reiter] did an edit on it after that. Whether it was actually Hermes or somebody else [editing] I don't know.

Don: And Hermes I love dearly, and you should see the way he edited material that I wrote to him, that went in, in revised form by Hermes. Because he felt he had to do it, and he's an honest guy. This is life.

Laurent: But I think that is vitally important. [In *Lord Meher*] if you are reading a block of words that you think are purely Meher Baba's words, I have personal experience that they are not. Unless by some magic the final edit got it closer to Meher Baba's words, which is usually uncommon.

Participant: But you're not talking about Meher Baba's words, you're talking about …

Another Participant: *Lord Meher*.

Laurent: I'm talking about *Lord Meher,* where there are big chunks of quotes from Meher Baba.

{talking in the background}

Laurent: I know that there are … I'm talking about direct experience that I've had with that …

Female Participant: Yes.

Laurent: … where I was horrified [that Meher Baba's words were edited].

Participant: So you are saying that the quotes are misquotes.

Laurent: *No, I am not saying that*. I am saying that they've gone through a process, where …

❡ Don: Of alterations …

Laurent: So, let's say Bhau took a diary from Chanji. Who knows what language Chanji wrote it in? But Bhau wrote his manuscript of *Lord Meher* in Hindi. Then Feram Workingboxwalla wrote [a translation of] that in English, and that was written up by David Fenster, and edited by Hermes. So what you're reading in *Lord Meher* has been through a process. It's very dangerous to think that Meher Baba said that exact word.

{a bunch of people speaking}

❡ Don: Today I say nothing on that. We've got enough on the table at the moment.

John: Are we as a group happier with say, Francis Brabazon's book *Stay with God*, which I believe is, people say, very faithful to the spirit of *God Speaks*.

❡ Don: I see no relation between the two. I think *Stay with God* is a beautiful book, Baba loved it, but to me it has nothing to do with the book that Baba gave out, *God Speaks*.

Norah: You mean the content.

John: I've heard people say …

❡ Don: Excuse me, I have to chop us off again for a few moments because we're getting awfully close to end of time and there is one other thing I just must bring up this afternoon. This is, let's say, the visions of different people of Baba. Here I think that the subject of unconscious contribution, or "coloring," of what is going on is extraordinarily important. The reason I wanted to bring it up now is because I want to ask Norah if she would say a few words on the coloring that can happen to, let's say, good straightforward visions. How much does my own personal subconscious, or ego, enter into what I see or what I think I hear?

Norah: Well, taking aside the question of whether you get a *real vision*, I'll put that aside for a moment.

Don: Sure, you put it anywhere you want.

Norah: Because it would probably be very rare.

Don: Um-hmm, it would be very rare.

Norah: But in the ordinary way, it would be almost impossible to separate out your own bent, your own way of looking at things, your own ...

Don: Your own unconscious contribution.

Norah: Yes, your own unconscious wishes. And, perhaps, the need for reinforcement of your own feeling about yourself. Even in dreams you can get, you can [trace] your own wishes, and your own unconscious feeling, let alone in a vision. And I think, yes, there may be truth in it, but it would have to be thought about in each individual case. What was going on in the person, and viewed with a *devil's advocate* approach for the most part. We would think of it [in this manner] as there is doubt to be cast unless it were proved otherwise.

John: So [conscious visions are] to be taken with several pinches of "sanskaric salt."

Norah: Yes.

Participant: What exactly are we talking about? The visions? Are we talking about anything concrete here? Are we talking about a person's visions?

Don: Anybody. Anybody who has visions of Baba.

Norah: Yes, one of us, yes, that's right.

Don: You and me, or even the remaining Mandali.

Rose: Can you cite any particular one, Don?

¶ Don: I'm not going to.

Rose: You're not going to. {laughter}

¶ Don: I refuse to. I want to keep this general. We're bringing up a generic problem, and getting a good expert's viewpoint on it, and I think we should take it seriously. But I don't want to focus it anywhere geographically, personalized, or anything of the sort.

Norah: All that I said was more from the psychological point of view, that there are these unconscious things and of course it has to do with sanskaras.

¶ Don: But we all have got our unconscious, don't we Norah?

Norah: But, the other thing is that this sort of vision, or thing, is not usually terribly important, even if it was true.

Participant: It would have very different significance than if Baba appeared to Eruch.

Participant: Oh yeah! Yeah.

Laurent: For who?

Participant: Very personal.

Participant: It would, generally.

Laurent: For whom would it have that [different significance]?

Male Participant: I believe generally it would.

Laurent: But what about for you?

Male Participant: For me, well I'm just saying we're talking about in a general, we say we're talking, this is just generally about visions. I believe qualitatively there is a great deal of difference between a vision that occurs to say, Eruch, than if a vision of Baba appeared to me.

Participant: Yes, but one would be of great importance to Eruch, it wouldn't be of importance …

Participant: No. I'm just saying that, if we're talking … In a sense I'm saying though that we can talk about it generally …

¶ Don: Laurent has his hand up.

Laurent: Well that definitely evoked something in me. For me the whole point is our own, personal journey back to union with Baba and whatever we need to get there. So if you had an experience of Baba *maybe it's exactly what you need,* and nobody else even needs to know about it. And it gets confusing when it's shared, sometimes.

Laurent also believes that some experiences are meant to be shared with others, and it does not matter whether it was experienced by a Mandali, or any one of us. For Meher Baba's sharing about experiences see *Discourses,* The Place of Occultism in Spiritual Life (Parts I, II, and III).

Participant: I have a feeling no one else would have … {several people laugh} From that point of view I think it is very different, so we can't talk about my vision and talk about Eruch's vision and say … it isn't the same thing. It's not.

Participant: Or Bal Natu's.

Participant: Indeed. Well, Bal, I'm just using Eruch. Eruch is no longer with us.

Participant: OK.

Male Participant: For that same reason … But uh-okay-but we're talking in code here, and I think, there is not a great deal of value, I don't think, in talking in code.

Don: There is another hand way back, Stevie.

Stevie Marions: How about, physical manifestations that a lot of people have had?

Participant: Like what?

Stevie: Or appear to have had, where Baba has actually been there in the room?

Participant: These are pretty rare, wouldn't they be? … like certain "once in your life" you would have that.

Stevie: Once you answer that question from a scientific standpoint does it have value, or is this all again something which …

Participant: From a scientific point of view? I'm not sure quite what you mean by *value* really there.

Stevie: I mean, is this more important than dreams?

Participant: Or only value, in the sense, if it has something to do with that particular person?

Participant: Could be very important for them.

Participant: What it means to them.

Stevie: I mean, is Don's original question, "What importance do we hold in store by these happenings?" Is that not really the point here?

Participant: No. I think the point is, where it is of value in the spiritual life really.

Stevie: Or how much *we* would have credence. But I think the original thing that Don posed was that people like the Mandali, who knew Baba in his lifetime, if they have dreams and manifestations, now how much they are important in our sort of future understanding, or in the history of it all? Whether that adds anything …

Participant: Whether they can be made more consistent? To apply to different people you mean?

Stevie: No. I'm just actually saying … The question surely that Don was posing was how much importance is this in terms of the resources available.

Participant: Ahh, yeah. But that's resources. That's what I mean. Are they *communicable* or are they just applicable to the person who has them. Because it's only a resource … to them.

Stevie: Does it just add to our breadth of vision that there "are more things in heaven and earth than are dreamt of"?

Participant: Oh, well yes.

Don: Well, Norah answered me, as a matter of fact, with her first sentence: that it's almost impossible to separate out your own unconscious contribution from let's say this type of an experience. You don't know how much your own subconscious has embellished the experience, and that is true in general, and even a Mandali is not safe from that. He has his unconscious, & Baba explained to me and made clear with what was going on with [William] Donkin, that right up to the end he [Baba] is working on sanskaric knots, even in the closest Mandali.

Participant: Well you might not think it has any relevance, but I was just thinking about the early Christians.

Don: No. I'm not saying, does it have any relevance ...

Participant: No. No.

Don continuing: But is it free from subconscious contact? [Coloring] Go ahead.

Participant: If you want to remember the early Christians ...

Participant: What you were going to say?

Participant: They all, as far as we know, pushed on the work quite literally, I mean the appearances of Christ in the closed room changed the disciples from being in a state of cowardly fear to going out to spread the gospel.

Participant: Yes.

Don: I would be much more inclined to accept something that happened to you and me and Norah and Laurent and Marion, than if it just happened to Don.

Participant: Yes. Yes.

Don: So if you've got a crowd of twelve pretty good people around, and they all agree on the same story, to me that's damned good evidence that it's not very much contributed to by subconscious personal additions.

Participant: Well it would be just as much, actually, if you get group action ... {general laughter}

Don: That's the advantage of having a professional. I'm going to suggest that ...

Participant: Can I just ask one thing, Don? *The Everything and The Nothing*, is it not the worked up response from Baba to questions after the publication of *God Speaks*?

❡ Don: Eruch said these were Francis [Brabazon's] writings from Francis' notes taken while Baba was talking with the [Delhi] businessman. That's the story precisely. That was Eruch, and I've never known Eruch to get confused on something like that.

Participant: So what do you have to say about it at all? You're just repeating Eruch's words.

❡ Don: I was boggled. I was boggled. That's all I've got to say. I think this is just typical of the sort of confusions that can grow up around the origins of a very important work. I think it's a terribly important work, but as far as I know about 90 percent of the people feel it's Baba's direct work, which it ain't. I mean, Eruch thought I was being ridiculous [when I assumed it was written directly by Baba].

Participant: So with the publication of *God Speaks,* there was no point subsequent to that where Baba was presented with questions that arose by those who read it.

❡ Don: Oh, well, an awful lot of people objected to an awful lot of things, but rather strange things.

Participant: People objected, but this want of clarification, having read *God Speaks,* that's not true?

❡ Don: There was a series of further questions put to Baba, which he then clarified, in the second edition. Because I was in charge of the second edition.

Participant: Yeah, so that's why I, No. No. No. There was a Supplement, which is, some sort of explanation to bits and pieces.

❡ Don: No. Questions that came up during the original editing of the first edition were sorted out and put into a separate volume by Ivy Duce, and they were taken directly from Baba's correspondence through Mani, but even that I do not give the same credence that I give the eight chapters of *God Speaks*, because the little – what was it –

Laurent: *Beams from Meher Baba on the Spiritual Panorama?*

Don: *Beans*. I think that was the one where she put them together. That was queries to Baba, answers from Baba to Mani, Mani typing up from her memory, and there is no evidence that she ever checked back and said, "Baba, read this and see if I got it straight." So the checking was not done, and so I don't give it the same value as the eight chapters of *God Speaks* where Baba told me clearly the story. OK?

Participant: Thank you.

Participant: What do you feel about [Bhau Kalchuri's book] *The Nothing & The Everything?*

Don: I have no comment.

After a discussion with Meherwan Jessawalla at Meherazad, on August 9, 2003, it became clear that the book, *Beams From Meher Baba,* is the book associated with *God Speaks*. Meherwan worked directly on *Life At Its Best* under Meher Baba's guidance, and clarified this point for us.

So, shall we be ... what I would like to do, if you will forgive me (this is being terribly selfish I know) but I'd like to do exactly the same thing that Baba did almost always at the end of the day with the Mandali. He would assemble them outside of Mandali Hall, facing Mehera's garden, and he would brace himself on Francis [Brabazon's] arm and he would give the *Master's Prayer* to Eruch, and Eruch would read it out. Nobody but Eruch would read out the *Master's Prayer*. So I was going to ask Norah if she would be our ...

Norah: No.

Laurent {To Don}: You should read it.

Don: No.

Norah: I should dry up.

Don: No. I always ... {To Norah}: You dry up? I can't imagine Norah drying up. If she says she's going to dry up, are you going to dry up?

Laurent {To Don}: You should read it.

Don: No. No. I never read it out loud. I always stood quietly at Baba's ... Baba had Eruch read it.

3 : Sunday Morning

LAURENT: SO IT'S SUNDAY, MAY 4TH. We're back at 228 Hammersmith Grove, at the Meher Baba Association, waiting outside for the meeting to start and it will start here soon.

{seminar starts with a song from Lol Benbow}

Don: {To Lol Benbow}: Can I delve just one moment into your subconscious? {Don looks questioningly at Lol, who has just played and sung an adaptation from South Pacific.}

Several participants: Go ahead.

Don: If Norah approves, that is.

Norah: What was that?

Don {To Norah}: I'm going to delve into his subconscious for one moment. {To Lol} That's the first time you ever played anything but …

Lol Benbow: "Begin the Beguine"?

Don: "Begin the Beguine" first. How come?

Norah: Nobody asked to play it.

Don: How come?

Norah: It was lovely.

Don: This is spontaneous. This is spontaneous. And I just wondered what prompted that, 'cause that …

Participant: This is a bit revolutionary.

Don: This is revolutionary. Yeah. Really. Anyway it just happens to be one of my very, very, very, very favorites. It's terrific. Yeah. Now can we do Baba's favorite?

Participant: I think we should. Shouldn't we?

⸿ Don: I think we should. Yeah.

{"Begin the Beguine" is played by Lol, followed by a Robert Bly version of a Kabir poem, read by John Horder}

John: For sure, we all know there is this phrase "The Guest", you'll all know who "The Guest" is.

{John reads aloud}

Friends, hope for The Guest while you are alive.
Jump into experience while you are alive.
Think and think while you are alive.
What you call salvation belongs to the time before death.
If you don't break your ropes while you are alive do you think
*   ghosts will do it after?*
The idea that the soul will rejoin with the ecstatic just because the
*   body is rotten, that's all fantasy.*
What is found now is found then.
If you find nothing now, you will simply end up with an apartment
*   in the city of death.*
If you make love with the divine now, in the next life you will have
*   the face of satisfied desire.*
So plunge into the truth.
Find out who The Teacher is.
Believe in the great sound.
Kabir says, when The Guest is being searched for, it is the
*   intensity of the longing for The Guest that does all the work.*
Look at me. You will see a slave of that intensity.

Participants: Jai Baba, John.

⸿ Don: Thank you, John. Jai Baba, John.

Participant: It's a really moving poem.

Participant: Oh, yeah, really, really moving.

⸿ Don: And John, you're going to wipe your eyes now cause

you're going to see The Guest. {To Alfred Saunders} Would you put it on? So I just wanted you to see Baba playing his drum, 'cause it's my favorite of all films of Baba.

{Don plays the video *Meher Baba at Home 1962*}

¶ Don: So now, everybody said when this came off of the press, "Don, it's got to be read out at the session when it starts." So here we are. A word before we start again.

A Word Before We Start

My job is to tell you what Baba told me about his manifesting; the Path of Love; the balance of head and heart and Don's "almost perfect balance between the two;" the gradual narrowing of the Path of Love; the role of his words; and the reason for all the Discourses on Meditation.

If I cannot tell you what he told me, and what he told me it was my responsibility to tell his lovers, then I will have failed my Beloved.

The story of the three bridges is my observation of how Baba ordered all this within our reference of time and space. I will describe this scenario now, but first, a simple recap of the larger picture I make out of what Baba has provided for us.

Meditation is the frame in the future within which Baba's gift of intuition to us will operate. And truing of this intuition is the contribution of the head and the companions bound by inner links. *God Speaks* is the great treasure by which intuition, within the frame of meditation, can unearth the riches of the Path.

"Read my words with your hearts open. Use the techniques of meditation I have given you for the frame of intuition for the spiritual charge I have attached to my words to flow into your being. After that, be content that I am one within you and will guide you on the course of your life."

Don: There we are. We've covered I would say almost two-thirds of the territory that I mentioned here [in the Agenda sheet] for yesterday. We've got a few points that have got to be done still, but before we go into it, one thing I've gotten used to on these two-day seminars is that when it's night time and I go to sleep, I wake up again somewhere around 3:30, and usually what I hear is, " Don, you forgot to do this, and you left out that, and that's not quite correct what you said there, so I quickly scribble some notes and try to get the thing all salted away and pushed together again for the second day. So this is my correction period, and the notes are all scribbled that I've got to take up.

The first one, Brendan, is: Brendan. Good Lord. I don't know if I can stand it. But you're looking calm and peaceful and smiling so let's try it anyway. So it was very simply, ah, Brendan, that you asked a very, very good logical question in relation to, "Why a translation of Baba's words if he has said, first of all, that he has attached the atomic bomb to the English ones [words], and that you don't have to understand two words in order to be able to absorb that [atomic bomb energy], and it will be a great help in your spiritual quest." And you said, well, then why all this business of translating them? Just give all the people who are interested in Baba a copy of the English originals and why all the hum and hurrah [of making translations]? He was much more polite than I'm being. Brendan always uses polite words to me. He never said a nasty thing yet, but he might today, when we get into this part of it. So Brendan sort of said, well you know, that's quite a bit of hum and hurrah and expense and so on, so just give them the English one. So then my little intuition was, why don't you ask Brendan why, if this is a feasible way to go about it, why did Baba spend so much time with you, Don, in working out, first of all, which are the three principal European languages, and then said now go ahead and get it [the three selected languages translations] done? So this is the early morning intuition back to Brendan. Do you have something to say there, Brendan? I thought it was a darn good counter question. I don't know why I didn't think of it [yesterday]. {general laughter}. Maybe I was battle fatigued by that point.

Brendan: I mean, I slip in and out of full presence here in the room.

¶ Don: You do.

Brendan: And, I'm not clear exactly what went on between yourself and Baba as far as requiring you, requesting you to deal with all the languages.

¶ Don: Yeah, that was when we had gotten done with several of those important projects that I was talking about. Baba was saying then to me, "Well, now you've been in America for quite awhile again and now you're back here in Europe, and what are your observations? What's going on in the spiritual world in Europe?" And I said, "Baba, it's a repeat of what went on with the four hippies in San Francisco, and they [the European hippies] are going to be knocking on the door for your words. I know it." And he said, "Well, that's an important point, Don. What are we going to do about it?" He asked me what are "WE" going to do about it? You know what he means by that, of course? What are you going to do about it? At any rate, we talked about what are the important languages? Well, there are a lot of different languages in Europe, and we can't do them all. So we talked about obviously French, because French is really a second ... at least at that time it was the second diplomatic language of the world, and tremendous numbers of cultured people knew French if they didn't know English. So we said, well, French has to be one, and then we went on.

It was well known that some of the principal publishing of

esoteric works in the nineteenth century had been in German editions. So, we thought, there's a lot of precedent there. A lot of scholars are very familiar with the German language publication of esoteric things and then we went on. What's the second great language in the world population? Why, it's Spanish, obviously. So, this was the rationale and Baba took time to go into all of this, Brendan. And he said, "Well, yes, what you say is right, and so these are the languages that are going to have to be done." And I said, "Well, you've got some awfully fine Baba Lovers in all three of those countries who will be capable of doing it." So, there he gets out his finger and points at me and says, "You do it." And I said, "But I'm just not expert enough to do that, Baba."

At any rate, this was Baba's approach. And you know, Baba was not a person for wasting motion and time so if, let's say, the logic of Baba attaching his spiritual bomb to the English edition is that you don't need to worry about whether you understand any of it, then why not just hand out the English edition? That's the end of story, and it's a lot cheaper, a lot less "kerfuffle" and hum and hurrah.

So my intuition was to ask you, Brendan, why do you think Baba, then, if that logic holds, and it's a workable, feasible path that will produce results, why do you think Baba spent so much time choosing three languages and then said to me, "You do it. No, you don't have to translate it, you can't, but you've got to supervise it." And I've spent a lot of time on it.

Brendan: Well, if you're putting a question to me directly, then the only answer can be in order to reach more people, that's the only thing I can think of.

¶ Don: So there's something about the mechanics then that isn't obvious in the logic of the situation. In other words the mechanics of how? How this thing can work out with real individual human beings in different countries, which the logic doesn't anticipate.

Brendan: … Baba knew what people were thinking.

¶ Don: Sure.

Brendan: Whether they were thinking in a given language is immaterial to Him.

¶ Don: Certainly immaterial.

Brendan: So much action is going on within a brain, that is, above & beyond language. If you're educated in the impression from a page of writing & the Atma … your consciousness, whatever, it's going to create an impression in the brain that's kind of the same impression, no matter what language you're reading.

¶ Don: Yeah. I had a chance for comparing a few notes with my pillar here at this side, Laurent, this morning, and I was telling him what I was going to start off with and where I would expect him to prompt me, which points, so he's aware of this. He said, "You know, that's an awfully interesting thing, and I've got a couple of thoughts." So I'd like to put Laurent on the spot and say, "Come on, get to it, boy."

Laurent: Well, that's why I'm here, I guess. One thing just came up, sitting here, which I haven't told you. It occurs to me that Baba, being the Master, always come down to the level of the disciple, or the student, and to require someone who doesn't speak the language to sit with *God Speaks* when they usually don't even sit with it in their own language, is a little bit much. The other question was … {To Brendan} I came up with a question for you. Do you speak French, Brendan?

Brendan: Well, it's difficult to say, unless you're French you don't speak French, but with that apart, yes, I do understand French and speak a little.

Laurent: OK. How about German?

Brendan: Yeah.

Laurent: Oh, very good. How about Portuguese?

Brendan: Now that's beyond me.

Laurent: OK. Good. What if you were in Portugal at a restaurant and the menu was in Portuguese, but you were very hungry and there was no translation for all the items on the menu, but everybody in the restaurant is very happy. They're all eating away. Why wouldn't you just say to the waiter, "Pick something off the menu," and say, "I'll just have that"? Usually the mind rebels when it is trying to do something that it doesn't understand. It wants to know what it is before it chooses, even though all we require is some food so that our body can keep moving. Right? It's like that, I think.

Brendan: Yeah.

Laurent: See?

Female Participant: I'd have a dictionary.

Laurent: Right. Well, or you'd ask the person, "What is that?" before you ordered it. I think it's kind of like that.

Female Participant: Or you might say, "I think I'll have the same as him."

Laurent: Right, sure.

Brendan: I don't know what the point is here.

Laurent: Translation. The value of translation is that it comforts the human personality that wants to know what's going on.

{conversation in the background}

Don: Wait just a moment, Norah's got the floor here. Go ahead, Norah.

Norah: No. I was only going to say that, Baba wouldn't leave us something that it is impossible to understand.

Don: No, he certainly wouldn't.

Norah: That three quarters of the world wasn't able to understand.

Laurent: Marion?

Marion Saunders: What I think he was saying, and I don't

know if Brendan understood it, but you're saying that reading it in another language you might get the energy but you
wouldn't know what is giving you the energy, so you'd like to
have a translation so you know what ... Say you read all in Portuguese, and feel this wonderful energy boost but you didn't understand a word of it. The same way, you might be eating food
but you don't know what you're eating. Using the translation,
well, you'll know what you're eating, and what is giving you the
energy boost. I think that's what you were trying to say.

Laurent: Yeah.

Brendan: I don't want to be misunderstood here. I am happy,
happy to learn that Baba was very specific in requesting you to
translate these works. It is undoubtedly an onerous task and *God
Speaks* is, without question, a dense piece of work. To translate
anything accurately is impossible. So I clear it on that basis.

You can make any translation you want once Baba said "Hey,
do this for me, Don." That's marvelous, but I also ... One of
the things that had me kick viciously against Catholicism a long
time ago was the requirement known specifically as ... otherwise you're out of the game. And that's blatantly unfair, and it
just didn't jell with me from a very early age.

Laurent: Isn't that another issue entirely?

Brendan: Well no. This is the business of – you don't need any
of these words to get there at the end of the day.

Laurent: That will come up at "the Three Bridges" won't it?

Don: I think it will. That's an important point.

Brendan: But having said that I wouldn't dream of knocking
the importance of what Don is on about.

Laurent: Sure.

Don: Sure.

Brendan: Because I'm coming around again, as far as I am
aware, and it is only the efforts that we put in here to get good

and accurate.

¶ Don: That is where the word "work" comes in, which is so key with ideas.

Brendan: Sure, Don, sure. These words are what I'm coming back to next time around.

¶ Don: David, you've got your hand up I think.

David Lee: I was thinking about something that was talked about yesterday in relation to Charles Purdom's book [*The God-Man*] about the relationship between "consciousness" and "awareness."

¶ Don: Awareness, yes. That's a terribly important point.

David: And it seems to me that to read a work in your own language, it begins to resonate within your own felt experience and your life.

¶ Don: You're saying it drills into your inner being in some way?

David: Yes.

¶ Don: When you say, "resonate," it's an important point.

David: So, that it's more easy to kind of apply into the day-to-day experiences that you're actually living through that have to be grappled with.

Participant: Really very important.

¶ Don: Yes. Could I bring up very quickly the word "attention?" Attention is necessary to do real work. How can you be attentive to something where you do not even know the language of the words? So there is an attention block that's involved here too. I feel simply Baba knows human mechanics and he knew what was necessary in order to get these words working, even if you didn't have to understand them intellectually, and apparently translation was part of the mechanics that he felt was absolutely necessary so he specified it and chose it carefully. David, go on.

David: I was thinking in terms of Catholic reference, that

shift that was made a number of years ago when you sang the mass in Latin, [and then] sang the mass in English. You know, that qualitative experience that people had in hearing the mass in their own language. It was quite an important step that was made.

Norah: Oral translation of the Bible.

Brendan: Don. It may just be a red herring, or whatever, I am just adding to David's point the fact that in the language of this country an awful lot of people suffered so that they could actually have the privilege of saying the mass that they used, *in their own language*. It didn't just happen. It was a long, long struggle against the authority of the Catholic Church which perhaps Baba tried to prevent this time, people having to suffer.

Don: He learns the obstacles to be avoided the next time around. Carol?

Carol Pullen: I think that is totally different, because the mass has music with it, and so the sound is acceptable to you in a totally different way from something that you read. So I would say that is a different question.

Participant: I would too.

Don: Is it back to me at this point?

OK. I have to tell you something that is terribly meaningful and important to me, and I think it very much pertains to what we are discussing now. When I went over to India last October (maybe it was even before that I can't even remember) there were three *God Speaks* seminars that were to be given in Bombay, Hyderabad and at Meherabad, and at each of those *God Speaks* seminars (at the end of them) what I call the "local bigwigs" would come up and say, "Oh, that's wonderful. It's so good to hear Baba's major book discussed, and it's all enlightening…" You know, they buttered me up, and they also brought in the wonderful work that Balaji had done in bringing out the Indian printed English [language] edition [of *God Speaks*] in India. It is a beautiful job and sold for three dollars and half so you got it desperately cheap, yet the quality is easily as good as the American edition on even better paper. Beautiful.

So after they had buttered Stevens, people would say, "Wasn't it wonderful that Balaji had this inspiration to make this available so people could have the book, because they couldn't afford it before, to have this book so they could read it for this wonderful seminar that we're having?" Balaji would smile and try to escape, because he hates attention. He's that way, he's a very shy guy.

Then, what happened? Point number three, and this was the important thing. When they got all of these niceties all done, at least two of them [the big-wigs present] would then look sort of wistful and they'd look me in the eye and say, "But it is so sad that there are millions of Indian Baba followers who are unable to read Baba's words at all because they're not translated into their languages. None of them suggested, you see, that somehow or other they ought to try to crack the English ones. This was said so soulfully and so realistically, and so I tumbled after it happened a third time – Well, Baba's trying to get a message over to me that the translating job isn't done yet even though we've practically finished the three languages for Europe, and he's pointing out now that we have to get busy on the Indian translations.

Then I began literally moving heaven and earth. This was a tough job, for a lot of reasons, to get people sort of conglomerated and to say, "Why don't we do something about it?" Then next, to get it funneled through the [Avatar Meher Baba] Trust and approved and signed and sealed. It was a monumental job, but it's done, and to me this is just obviously the extension of Baba's will: *translating meaningfully His words*.

I don't mean to snowstorm this thing, but this to me was very meaningful, and it's exactly what we're talking about here.

Laurent: Just one final point on that, I believe Baba said his wish was that *God Speaks* be translated into as many languages as possible.

Don: Well, it's being translated into as many languages as possible. It is quite true.

Laurent: Yeah.

Don: Because after those three had been done, remember I told you yesterday, the Trust …

Participant: {interrupting with a comment to Laurent}

Laurent: No. I believe that was what exactly he said, "As many languages as possible."

Don: {continuing} … The Trust gave me the assignment outside of India to be responsible for vetting and giving approval for the translation of Baba's books, all of their copyrighted books, and the Sufis [of Sufism Reoriented] roughly have given an equivalent right in some of these languages, too. So, Baba's wish is being done. It's being followed through.

I wanted to go on with my morning intuition notes, but they frankly dropped off the planet somewhere or another! I don't know where they went. I was looking for them here. I had them in with what we call a trombone [French for paper-clip] to my papers here.

Marion: Oh, they're there.

Laurent: There they are.

Don: Oh, Marion. Isn't that interesting.

Marion: Did you give them to me, Don, this morning? {she laughs}

Don: Yeah. Go ahead, Brendan, please.

Brendan: Oh, I'm just wondering, since your concern is for accuracy as far as what's attributed to Baba and what is Don. Is there a place for a concise *God Speaks*, chapters one to eight? You can cut the rest out.

❡ Don: No, we didn't. No. When we were talking about translating Baba's words.

Brendan: Not in translation. The English version. Why does it contain so much extraneous material as far as you can tell?

❡ Don: Because that was given to Murshida Duce as her option. A free will offering from Baba to keep the supplement and include it, to eliminate it entirely, or to pick out certain sections. And Murshida Duce then exercised her options and said, "I want it all." So this was Baba's gift to her and I don't know anybody who would, let's say, try to countermand that in any fashion, Brendan. It's not the question. It's never come up, to tell you the truth. The only time a question comes up is when people get annoyed with me because I pointed out that the Supplement [to *God Speaks*], which is a huge part of it, does not have the stamp of authority of being Baba's loaded words. So, some people feel that is ... What should I say? They say, "Well, Baba's name is on the whole thing, doesn't that mean Baba knew all about it and approved of all of it?" I simply cannot say that follows the criteria that Baba so carefully explained to me of what have these atom bombs of spiritual energy attached. That's the difference. But I would never dream of cutting it out, Brendan, just to be simple.

Brendan: Then what about a sentence in there? Just as you've described there. The loaded words are chapters one to eight.

❡ Don: One to eight.

Brendan: And I think that'd be a bit tricky because there are plenty of Prefaces. One Preface is as good as two or three there.

❡ Don: Uh-huh.

Brendan: There's a Preface for each edition [actually Introduction – *Ed*], and I don't know which edition we're up to now. So that in the next printing, is there not a scope for an addendum for that fact?

❡ Don: To leave them out or ...

Brendan: No. No. Just as you said, "Baba's loaded words are kept as one to eight."

⁋ Don: Yeah.

Laurent: Oh. To say that … Put that in …

⁋ Don: Actually, Brendan, that has been suggested on a couple of occasions, but then immediately turned down by people in an authoritative position who think – No, this was put out in Baba's lifetime. – The only thing that has been changed since then … Well, there have been things that were started to be changed while Baba was still alive, and I had my questions to put to him about things we might change. So, edition number two, where there are modest changes that were made, was virtually all carefully taken up with Baba himself.

The Introduction to the second edition was written by me, except for about two paragraphs, which Murshida Duce and Lud [Dimpfl] wrote. But all of that then went through India and was approved, of course. When I heard any suggestions, I simply passed them on.

Now you suggest, "Why don't we leave some of the extraneous material out for simplicity's sake and just keep the loaded parts?" Immediately everybody would say, "No, the major decision in relation to what's included in *God Speaks* was given by Baba to Murshida Duce. Murshida Duce made the critical decision. Let's leave it that way."

The assignment [to Don], incidentally, of writing the Preface and the first Introduction was passed through Baba, and he very carefully had my words read out to him. I might say, Brendan, the report Mani gave me: "He thought they were terrific!"

{everybody laughs} That's a sheer aside.

{To Laurent}: I hope you didn't get that on tape. It's shocking to have this passed down. An example of gross egotism.

Brendan: Take it easy, Don.

Don: Yeah.

{Some humorous chiding between Don and Brendan}

Brendan: Don, I'm very sorry to learn that you're having problems with authority.

Don: Don't we all, Brendan! Yeah.

Brendan: Well, I'm very sorry to learn that you're having trouble with your ego.

Don: Well, it sticks around, Baba warned, until you get on the seventh plane. So I guess it's here to be troublesome a little while longer. At any rate, we've got two things that I think we have to try to get done before we chug back into the outline here, and this is a lot of material that we've got to get through today. There's some real tough and awfully exciting work. But I've got a few more notes on intuition, and actually Laurent has reminded me that my intention yesterday was to completely leap to the back [of the agenda] and raise the question of what is all this business about bridges and the "third bridge?" Because that is the reason we are here. Because we are in something already which I call "the third bridge era" of Baba's transmission of his message to humanity.

Laurent: At least an overview.

Don: I'll tell you very, very quickly. After I had met Baba he said, to me, "Well, Don, there are a lot of people who know me and love me scattered around the world. You're in international petroleum and you jump around the world, so make a point of seeing some of these people. It will probably be interesting and delightful for you to know them." So, I did just that, and the thing that was unexpected to me was that when I'd see this or that person and meet people like Hedi Mertens and so on, always they had saved things about Baba that they had picked up. Many times I would find that they had little pamphlets about Baba and quotations from Baba I had never seen. I remember reading in one of those, I don't know where it was for heaven's sake, but one of the things that I read that really touched me went something like this: *Yes, I say I am the Avatar, and that is an important position. It is an important charge. But I want you to know that even the Avatar is only the bridge to Reality, which is God.*

That made a hell of an impression on me. Because I knew Baba by that time, and I knew what a terrific bridge he was, what a terrific individual he was. And simply, then, to read what this being, who had all of the qualities that I could never imagine a human being having, right there in the flesh breathing in front of me, and have him say that, "I'm just a bridge to Reality." It absolutely, as Keith would say, "It blew my mind." It really did. I was so touched.

Participant: I only wanted to say, it used to be one of the Christian appellations that he was the bridge.

¶ Don: Well, I probably hadn't done enough on my religious (on my Christian religious) background, because it was the first time I ever came across something like that. So there I was, terribly impressed. Then years later, as I got through the *Discourses* I saw in there that Baba also says, "Yes, I say that I am God, but truly you are God too. The only difference between us is I know that I am God and you do not yet know it."

That also impressed me tremendously, that the Avatar himself, you know, would say, – Look, yes, I'm a big shot, but I'm not the only shot, and the really big shot is where you're aiming yourself at, and that's the important business that's got to be done – So, that too really touched me tremendously. And the word "bridge" was key.

Strangely enough, when I was starting to prepare the outline for all of these seminars, something came to me about the *Judas function in our time*, and this is also a terribly important item.

Laurent: We have to pick up the pace.

Don: Yep, we gotta pick up the pace. The whip-cracker is brief.

Brendan: That's just to say that is why Baba's diagrams are important.

Don: Yeah, terribly important, Brendan.

Brendan: Also isn't that why the Muslim faith again today is saying there can be no representation of God that does not belittle God, and therefore is a nonsense ultimately as a concept, that you can't represent God. Even to call God, "God" is to belittle God.

Don: Well, of course Baba says essentially to us again and again and again that there is no way you can get to grips with this until you become God yourself. But, nevertheless, we've got an awful lot of homework to do in getting along the way, and that's where we are now. But to get back to the bridges and just to give you an overview of what we're going to be taking up most of the rest of the day this concept of the "bridge," ...

Participant: I have at least recognized it is about bridges.

Don: Yes, it is about bridges. As I was starting to do all of this [work on he seminar] I picked up a book that our publisher in Spain had given me, which he had written on Jainism. There is nothing on Jainism in Spanish, strangely enough, and I had this sitting by my bedside for a year and a half and thinking – Gee, I've got to get into this – and for some reason or another as I started to draft the outline for this, I just happened to pick this up and start to read it and I said, "My God, this guy is a good writer. It's terrific stuff that he's doing. I'm not interested in Jainism, but he knows his subject and he presents it so interestingly." Then on pages about ten to fifteen, I managed to get there my Spanish stumbling along with me, all of a sudden I got into the Jain concept of the "Bridge to God." It was terrific, and it was so beautiful and it was so simple and I said, "Well, there it is again. I wonder if this came from part of Baba's background in mysticism when he was a little kid in India, the concept.

The word "bridge" has got a lot of mystic significance. It wasn't just my reading that little chance article where Baba says – I'm just a bridge to God, that's my only function. – It's a major, major mystic concept and I had known nothing about it. It goes back thousands of years apparently. So, isn't it interesting how Baba brings up these resources when you really need them? Now we're going to be talking about the bridge, and this has tremendous reality, and I had heard Baba say that [in his writings], and then I had tumbled to the fact that the Mandali were "The Second Bridge," and saw how beautifully they functioned as the second bridge when Baba was not here in the flesh.

There are certain things that the flesh has to do to bridge over for us and, by heaven, they did just that. Then I began reflecting on the fact, well, the Mandali, you know, now it's just so obvious they're almost gone, they're almost finished. So I said, "Well, where's the third bridge going to be?" But then I began to be aware of the fact that something strange was happening to *God Speaks* and, you might say, people's acceptance or interest in it. Then I began to say, "I wonder…" Then all of a sudden I said to myself, "My Sainted Aunt Minnie! Baba's words are obviously, from all of the things that he said to me, and the importance of his *words*, these are going to be a main strut in the third bridge. The Third Bridge which goes on until he comes back again." This is a terribly important concept.

One of the most important things from all of that, though, arrived as I was getting this down and sending it out to two or three people whose comments I value greatly on such subjects. Back came one or two comments like, "Don, are you sure that isn't too centralized and narrow: Baba's words - and that is it?" Then again, early one morning, one of those intuitions, and I just had sort of a vision. There's a bridge (Third Bridge), nice great big steel girders, you know, bearing a lot of load, and here's a train going across, and the train is loaded with people. It's got a dining car on it with a buffet lunch spread out, and in the dining car there are a lot of people helping themselves. There's a principal hot dish in the center of the buffet table, and the principal hot dish is labeled "Baba's words." But there are all sorts of other dishes spread around here, of things that Baba has given us, and that mysticism has given us, and which are terribly important for this meal which is going to take place on the third bridge.

We'll go over some of those, too, as a matter of fact. But I am convinced that the principal hot dish in that dining car on the third bridge is Baba's words. And that's one of the real reasons why I wanted to be sure we took it up in these seminars.

{To John}: Well, John, I'm not going to be able to get to the neutral plateau and hugging this morning. Isn't that shocking? Yes, it is, because I suddenly realized recently the extent to which Baba utilized hugging, because I got quite a few of those hugs.

And then I began experimenting and saying, "What's all this hugging business about?" You know, and I think many of you realize that the hugs I give you have got quite a bit of language in them. There's quite a bit of exchange that goes on. They're not just sort of nice little bear hugs, they're terribly meaningful.

Finally I said to myself, "Wow, I see now why Baba did it, and what he was utilizing." But I never dared tell John Horder my suspicions, and some of the things I found out about all this, because I knew it would send him over the moon, and I don't know if we'd ever get him back from there again. He's already so addicted to the subject you see. But maybe we'll get time this afternoon to go on with the rest of that and the neutral plateau. The neutral plateau fits in to all of that as well, strangely enough.

Now I think we've just got to … we've only taken half of our morning already.

[Laurent] is going to crack the whip again if we're not careful. He can be severe. Remember he is a shaker and a doer, so we've got to do things. Did you happen to read, have any of you taken any time and passed by that bountiful crop of paper that we've got strung up on the back of this door here, which has the agenda for our two days? Well, I have to read one line to you which is the line to start the second day.

Uh, oh … {Don tries to find a note}

❧ Don: {referring to the paper he has been looking for} It simply says, "The Judas function in our time." Now of course everybody is very familiar with the word "Judas," and an awful lot of people have done a lot of speculating on whether Judas would show up and what sort of clothes he'd be in and what sort of job description he would have this time around, because Baba said, "I always have the same Mandali around me performing the same function." So we've got it straight from the horse's mouth: there's got to be a Judas somewhere, and nobody has been leaping out of the woodwork to claim the title for himself, so what do we think about it?

Participant: Are we surprised?

❧ Don: Are we surprised? Well. Not a great surprise. If I were Judas, I would certainly try to hide, but … Norah, you were about to say something.

Participant: We would have to be veiled if we were.

❧ Don: We'd have to be veiled.

Participant: We'd all have to be veiled.

❧ Don: Yes. Right. Brendan.

Brendan: Judas is a grievously misunderstood character …

❧ Don: We're not going to go into that yet, Brendan. Can you hold the comment until I give what the historical background of that line was? Why it came up? Because I've got to get that off my chest. You remember, I've been very frank with you, because it came up just before we went to work here, that I had the third episode when words formed in my mind when I was doing some intuitive work. And I just said to myself these words: "I recognize the manner in which words are used. This has got to be straight from Baba, for whatever reason, that it's coming through this way."

I'm not prone to these things. I hate revelations, to be perfectly honest with you. But if there is something about which I just have to say to myself, "This has got all of the earmarks, the way Baba used words, and the way he handled things," I've got to take this very seriously. That's happened to me three times. The third one was that paragraph [that was read out in *A Word Before We Start*], and I think it's a monument of a paragraph. I can't claim it.

The second time that I had this experience was when a lot of things were going wrong with the various projects that I was involved in, you know, words, Baba's words, translations, additions, and so on, trying to be careful that the sense and the meaning of Baba's words is properly preserved. This has been my life for a long time. And on this occasion I was very upset. Now, I do a daily report out loud, as you all know, to Baba (that came from a long story we won't go into, but it's important to me). And when I make my daily report I do not ask Baba questions; I do not ask Baba instructions or advice. This is a no, no, taboo-land for me. I carefully avoid it. I'm simply doing what he told me to do: "Give me a report on the principal things of your life. Do it regularly, and do it by the most handy physical means possible."

My voice is the handiest, so I do it out loud. I tried thinking them, you know, and it just didn't work, because that isn't a physical means. Thought is different.

At any rate, this is what I've been doing for years, and on one occasion (it was two, three years ago) I was suddenly so upset by a lot of cockeyed things just going plain wrong with things that Baba had given me as a responsibility, and I just suddenly burst out in my room, I think I was in a hotel somewhere on a field trip again, and just said, "Baba, for heaven's sake, what is going on here? What's the meaning of this?" I was distressed. I said this. I don't do this sort of thing with Baba. I was shocked at myself when the words came out of my mouth. And you know, I was not asleep, hadn't been asleep. Simply, very clearly and simply, the words formed, and I'm not going to tell you all of the words, but the gist of them was that *the Judas function in this incarnation of the Avatar related to the betrayal of Baba's Word*. The Word, and not the body. Now this is an unusual concept, isn't it?

So this is the second reason for suggesting these seminars. I said, "Good heavens, this is important and I can see what is going on. I can see, really, the danger to which Baba's words are being subjected already. I know his words." And so on, and I see so many crazy things happening in so many directions. And it upsets me, and I said, "Certainly, one of the things I've got to try to do is to set out what I know about Baba's words." But here is the real work in what I see that we are dealing with now, and I have experience with myself in seeing how easy it is [to make serious errors], even though I was born and bred and weaned by Baba himself on how his words are given out, and the importance of keeping them right and straight. I've seen Don Stevens pull some really cockeyed things. I know how mortal we are, and how terribly careful we have to be.

Laurent: It requires a discipline.

Don: This requires discipline, absolute discipline. And it also requires – what's that lovely word that Norah loves to use? Norah says one of the chief functions of a civilized person is discretion. Yes. Discipline and discretion.

Norah: Discrimination.

¶ Don: Discrimination. Discrimination. Yes. I love Norah for bringing that word out every once in awhile & reminding us that this is our responsibility to Baba. Discrimination. Gosh. Discipline & discrimination. Kavita, what would you do for us now?

Kavita: Well, to me it's *the Judas function*. I have some questions about that. Why is it necessary to have that in Baba's incarnation? Because that's an assumption.

¶ Don: Why is it necessary?

Laurent: An assumption?

Kavita: I think it's an assumption.

Laurent: *Baba said it.*

Kavita: Baba says that there is a Judas function?

Laurent: Around him. Yes.

Kavita: OK. Then if that's the case then, from what I've known and felt, the function of Judas was during Jesus' life, it was to carry out what his will was. So within the divine plan, even though it was contradictory – I mean it was seen as the wrong thing to do – I think it was what was *meant to be done* along the way.

¶ Don: What was necessary.

Kavita. Yes. So it would actually defeat the purpose, the long-term goal. *So if Baba said that it's necessary, I mean, the Judas function is working in his incarnation, then I would say that it would be something that's necessary to fulfill his ultimate divine purpose, whatever it is, and it's not necessarily a negative thing in the long term.*

¶ Don: Kavita, we know each other well enough so you will allow me to say I think you're absolutely dead spot right. That's chapter two, and chapter three is to avoid the consequences of that betrayal. And that's our responsibility.

Laurent: Can I say a word?

¶ Don: Yes. Please do.

Laurent: Are you familiar with the *Ramayana*? The story of Lord Rama?

❡ Don: Yes.

Laurent: Baba indicated that in that incarnation as Lord Rama, Ravana, who is called *the demon*, who kidnapped his wife Sita, played the role of Judas. And of course they fought this war over Sita. {To Kavita}: Which side would you join in that fight, or would you just watch? Most of us would want to fight along side Lord Rama, because he is the Avatar. But some chose to fight along side Ravana. And yet, it was all in the plan obviously. Somebody had to play that role, for that *tension* to be there, and God only knows what the work was, that was done through all that drama. Right? I think that it is important that we choose our allegiance. Does that make sense?

❡ Don: Stevie, I think you were …

Steven: No, I just think that was quite fascinating, actually.

❡ Don: Yes, it's tremendously important, if the words that I heard in the back of my mind are from Baba, if that represents the situation, then we have a tremendously important mutual responsibility before Baba.

Marion: It's a big responsibility, isn't it?

❡ Don: It's a responsibility. This is Keith's word, responsibility.

Alfred: Well, in our group, that's necessary. That's every day, every minute.

❡ Don: It is. You couldn't have put it better, Alfred. It is minute-by-minute responsibility.

Participant: How can we possibly know?

❡ Don: Become aware. Become aware of what is going on, first of all. And then start reflecting. And then start acting. Start responding.

Participant: How come … I mean, you know so much of Baba's words, but how can, in people like me, who have … I've read a certain amount, but I haven't read everything. And how can I know what is really Baba's words? Is that what you're saying, that somehow it's getting slightly distorted?

¶ Don: Yes.

Participant: People arguing about what he really said. What he didn't really say.

Laurent: No. It's worse than that. *They are changing Meher Baba's words even.*

Participant: Oh, really? And then publishing them?

Laurent: Oh, yes.

Participant: So how can, how can you know?

Laurent {To Don}: Sorry, I'll let you …

¶ Don: Fight!

Participant: But how can I know which is right, and which is wrong? I mean …

¶ Don: Refer back to Baba's words. If you see them being reprinted and re-quoted somewhere or another & something says to you, "Gosh, this seems a little strange. Is this really Baba?" Go back and find those words, as he did them originally, and then say, "No, this is misquoted, and that thing ought to be withdrawn from publication."

Participant: Can you tell me which are absolutely Baba's words, so I can refer to them?

¶ Don: We did that yesterday, and I'm delighted to go over them again today. Yes. There's no question at all in my mind, the first eight chapters of *God Speaks*, Baba himself had Eruch explain to me twice how they were given by Baba, and that is the prototype for all. When Baba gave me a little sheaf of papers at the end of the first language group of the Four Language Sahavas, he indicated to me that all of these papers that he was giving, which is part two of *Listen Humanity*, he had given out in precisely the same manner that he had given out the eight chapters of *God Speaks*, to Eruch. Then I found out later on, through Adi Irani, that the "Song Of The New Life" had been given out by Baba in exactly the same fashion and then double checked by Baba: not just once finally before it was given out, but a second time.

Those I know for absolute certainty. That is the bedrock. That's a lot of material already. In addition to that, and here I just have to admit my own ego preferences and sanskaras, I love the *Discourses*. I've used them. I've seen how they have been used. But Baba did not tell me at any time that they had been handled the same way as he handled *God Speaks*, or part two of *Listen, Humanity*, or "The Song Of The New Life." I love [The *Discourses*]. I think that they fulfill a unique position for Baba followers. And I am also dead certain, because I have seen the manner in which Baba himself used "O Parvardigar" and the "Prayer of Repentance", I know those also have to be exactly the same sort of thing. Those I know absolutely, indelibly.

Laurent: But Don, since I'm sitting here …

Don: Yes?

Laurent: I can't let you off the hook that easily. You know something about the …

Don: {interrupting Laurent} I think we're going to get Norah back here and just relax! {laughter abounds} You stay right here. He's a tough son of a gun {indicating Laurent to the audience}. You know, my affectionate name for him is "The little bear." He's got sort of these bear qualities, but when I get a little impatient with him I say, "Hey, you Big Moose." {more laughter} So now he's being the Big Moose, and he's still got to sit here. {To Laurent}: Go ahead.

Laurent: Well. I have to, I have to answer to Baba.

Don: You do. You answer to Baba.

Laurent: And ah, you know something …

Don: Put me in my place now.

Laurent: Well.

Don: Go ahead.

Laurent: No. Because we've talked about this.

Don: Yes.

Laurent: You know something about the Sheriar version of the *Discourses* that I can't just sit here comfortably & let that go by.

⁊ Don: Oh, God! Why does he have to bring that up today?

John: It has to be. It has to be.

⁊ Don: I suppose it does.

John: I was going to bring that up. It's ... it's ... I mean I've got something to read from the old *Discourses* now, that hasn't been marked up in the [new] one volume [7th edition].

⁊ Don: Well, all right. So I'm on the spot, and I do have to say something, as Baba explained what honesty is, and how we had to follow it in our vow to him. It is perfectly true that when, let's say the Mandali were getting older, all of them decided that there must be a final re-editing of the *Discourses* – done while some of them who had been around Baba, and his thoughts, were still there.

Laurent: After Baba dropped his body.

⁊ Don: After Baba dropped his body. This was a Mandali decision that was made. And it was decided, I think most of you are familiar with the fact, that Eruch, Bal Natu, with Chris Flagg, or Flagg Chris, I never remember which, was to be, you might say, the secretary of this situation. So that was done. I found out about this early, just accidentally, because I'm terribly close to Eruch. I kept seeing him through the years and we'd talk about things related to Baba's words, and what was going on.

Eruch worked very hard with Bal Natu and Chris Flagg for a long time. *Remember this*, though, I have to say Eruch was still a human being. He still had some wedges of sanskaras and Baba would occasionally get after him. So, even Eruch was fallible, but Eruch was the chief person to suggest various different things. Bal Natu much less. And then the two sort of turned it over, secretary-wise, to Flagg Chris. Flagg Chris is a superbly trained academic librarian, and he knows his business. And he is a good master of words, too, and he knows proper sentence structure.

Flagg then began going through what had been gone over by Bal Natu and by Eruch, and he began correcting it from a grammatical standpoint. I get along well with Flagg because I like him, I think he's a good workman. And he would send me material and suggestions and so on. His editorial changing I would never have done, and I called that to his attention. He went through editorial changes number one, which were partly supervised by Bal Natu, but not by Eruch. Then, finally, he started going through for a second time. At that point, Sheriar threw up their hands and said, "We accept no more changes, we've got to get this thing out and printed."

Hence there were changes made that were not supervised by either Bal Natu or Eruch and still further ones that were in the mill when Sheriar called time out. This is the story. You draw your own conclusions. As a result there is quite a vast difference, finally, between the little three volumes, which I edited under Baba's supervision, and then the Sheriar [seventh] edition. There is quite a great deal of difference. I'm not going to sit around and bellyache about it. But it's an important story, and I have probably the only existing copy which has all of Chris Flagg's unsupervised changes marked in red, so I think that's an important document.

Laurent: And it's not a little red.

⸮ Don: It's a lot.

Laurent: Too much.

⸮ Don: Because he is a good academician. He knows academic proper English structure.

John: Well, it made a lot of difference.

⸮ Don: It makes a great deal of difference in the styling.

Participant: But also the meaning? Not the meaning?

¶ Don: Well, some people claim the meaning in important places has been changed.

Laurent: Or even a comma, can change the meaning.

Participant: Yeah.

¶ Don: I think Keith was ... Oh, excuse me. Davie, you were waving first.

David: No, I was just moving on to the "Song Of The New Life" and the two different versions that ...

¶ Don: Isn't that incredible? See what Purdom himself did? He reversed the meaning of "Let your garden be destroyed ..." because you're going to rebuild it. He said [instead], "Don't let your garden be destroyed." Purdom! Dependable Purdom.

Laurent: He didn't like it.

¶ Don: God! He said, obviously this is a mistake.

Participant: He couldn't believe it.

Don. He couldn't believe it. No. Literally he couldn't believe Baba would say such a thing. Just simply, simply put. But this is what we are dealing with. And this is important. Davie, what do you want to add?

David: So in publications where the "Song Of The New Life" is in print, is it "Let your garden ..."?

¶ Don: You find them both ways now.

David: You find them both?

¶ Don: Yes. You find them both.

Participant: What's the correct version?

¶ Don: Purdom did it: "Let not your garden be destroyed." Baba put it: "Let your garden be destroyed ..." Because ... you will totally renew it.

Participant: Just the opposite

¶ Don: Totally.

Participant: Yeah. The words that follow it are, "You beautify it again by your ..."

❡ Don: Then that makes sense doesn't it? But it's a pretty rugged thing to think about – Let the boa constrictors tear up all the trees – you know. Gosh! I don't know if boa constrictors tear up trees. {laughter} Have you ever seen them in your … ?

Laurent: That one needs a little help, Don.

❡ Don: I'm sure Paul [Gregory] will get a design out for me on this one, on his graphic artistry. Let's have a good one, on that one, Paul. Boa constrictors & trees uprooted. Anyway, where are we?

Laurent: Can I give a couple-more examples since we're in this mode?

❡ Don: We're right in this mode and it's important.

Laurent: One thing that bothers me, somebody may say, "Oh, it doesn't matter," but this really bothers me. When Baba's quotes are taken from many different places, many different sources, and then strung together one after another as if Baba said it all in one sitting, and then published like that without any indication that they're taken from other sources. No footnotes. Nothing about sources. And then it looks like Baba just sat and gave this little thing.

Participant: Which book is that, Laurent?

Laurent: Oh, there's numbers of them.

Participant: Give me one.

Laurent: Sure. *Meher Baba's Call*. That little book that many people love.

Participant: Strung together?

Laurent: Oh, yeah. Oh, yeah.

Participant: But, it's taking out of context …

Laurent: It's worse than that. Taking a quote out of context can be dangerous alone. But taking a number of quotes out of context and stringing them into one context, without letting anybody know that, can be really confusing …

❡ Don: Mary.

Mary Turner: But how about if the power of Baba's word, you know Baba's words are in there somewhere, his power, his love, his reaching out to us, is in there somewhere, it's going to get to us, you know, it's going to reach us.

Laurent: I'm not disagreeing with that. But why not just put each quote with maybe some notes, you know footnotes, or something at the bottom, and put a little [decoration] between each quote?

Don: So a person can orientate themselves. Relate it to a source.

Laurent: And if they really like the quote, they can go back to the material and say how, in what context, did Baba even say this? Did he say it to an individual? Did he say it at a mass darshan [program]?

Mary Turner: But the feeling I'm getting here is, I'm … you know, *my whole sort of Baba-thing is sort of dissolving before my very eyes.* {Mary's voice sounding very emotional} *I mean, I just love Baba, you know, and all of those words at some time have reached me and touched me. And, you know … I know what you're saying, and there's an academic thing that needs to be done very definitely. But, you know, don't let's forget that Baba loves us. I mean he just wants us and that's all that really matters.*

Laurent: Absolutely.

Marion: I was brought up on the first edition, *Meher Baba Calling*, and that's how I learned to love Baba. They were put together by a person of great love, and they were like, musically put together by that person's heart.

Laurent: True.

Marion: Somebody came along, reprinted it, retranslated them, and all the music and love essence have gone out of them. And it was just horrible. You know. Somebody's trying to say, " I get to make with this … " with their mind correct … and then try to alter and add. And it's very strange because there was music, hidden music, in the first edition, which was put together very thoughtfully by somebody's heart that could hear that music.

Laurent: Sure.

Marion: So, you've got to realize some people have a lot of skill in what they do and then somebody comes along and they say, "Oh, can't hear that music. And it's incorrect. I must correct this." It's like correcting somebody else's musical piece … and adding something …

Laurent: Sure. I want to respond to something. {To Mary Turner}: I don't know your name.

Don: Mary … Turner.

Laurent: Mary Turner. Mary, I just want to respond by saying I agree wholeheartedly with what you're saying, and I actually believe Baba is so forgiving that people were doing this in his lifetime with their love, their full blown love for Baba was doing this all of the time, and he was just so happy with their love that he did not necessarily call them before him and say, "What are you doing with my words?" Right? Don is saying that.

Participant: But you are saying that we have to be watchful.

Don: You have to be watchful. I'm saying that.

Other Participant: Yes, definitely.

Laurent: Yes. But Baba is so forgiving. All he wants is our love. Just like you said. Right? But it is different now. It's a little different now. *Because we are the custodians of his word.*

Kavita: Ah, yes. Can I respond to that? We are the custodians of *his love* and the way we love one another is his love traveling, you know, beyond his lifetime and into the future. And we constantly tell one another what Baba says, and how to be, and what Baba thinks. I mean, you know, it's only, it's love, and if we use his words to try and tell each other how it is, but that's not, it's the thread of love that communicates, not what we say.

Don: I think Richard had his hand up about the same time.

Richard Turner: I just wanted to just clarify whether the issue here is … I mean, are we saying, are we putting forward the proposition we should all be watchful and mindful of these changes? Or are we saying that there should be guardians of these words, and there should be people in charge?

Don: Well, I've argued with myself a number of times about the same thing, Richard. When the day is done, I always come back to the feeling that it's our total, all of us, responsibility. We all have to be watchful and mindful. And I don't think that any person can say, "Well, I've got to be two hours a day watchful and mindful," and another person say, "Well, twenty seconds a day is about all I'm good for," but it is a total responsibility for people who love Baba. He emphasized so many times to me, constantly, the importance of his words and the care with which he expected me to handle them, and how he had handled them with Eruch, principally. I just want to see that a proper line of care continues, and that we don't all go just sort of bananas and say, "Well, it's great." Because it is not great. There is real responsibility that's got to be exercised. Go ahead Richard.

Richard: *I'm very heartened to hear that, Don, because the thing that I'm really worried about is whether there needs to be some sort of priest class. "Only they know …"*

Don: Bless your heart. It would certainly be the last thing Baba wanted, and by …

Laurent: I'd leave right now.

Participants: {many remarks in the background}

Don: He didn't make me a priest, but he certainly laid down the hard line. He laid it down gently to me, but it was a very workman-like line that he constantly harped on.

Laurent: I think {pointing} here, and then Chris, and then David and then Brendan, because we haven't heard ...

◄ Don: Good heavens, then it's lunchtime. So, I'm going to go have my lunch now.

Laurent: Is that OK?

◄ Don: Yes. Right.

Participant: Just as a very brief observation, and we only have to look at what has happened with the words of *The Bible*, for example, and the changes that were made there at later times, or *The Koran* to see the importance of what you're actually saying here.

Laurent: And Baba indicated the same. He said every scripture of major world religions has been altered by the priests for their own selfish ends.

Participant: Look at the problem of reincarnation, for example, in *The Gospels*.

Laurent: [Reincarnation is] gone.

Participant: It's gone.

Participant: So it was earlier. {other comments in background}

Chris Gray: This brings up a huge, important issue.

Laurent: Why don't you come [closer] up here, Chris?

Chris: {saying something ... probably indicating he doesn't want to come up}

◄ Don: He's more comfortable there.

Chris: A couple of years ago I was in India and I started asking people, "Do you know what these three words actually mean: *darshan*, *prasad*, and *sahavas*? And I went, possibly went through a dozen people.

Laurent: Westerners?

Chris: Westerners and Easterners, and I think an elderly Indian [woman] actually was the only person who came up with the original, literal meaning of these words. Do you know what they mean?

Laurent: Who are you asking?

Chris: Anybody.

Don: I'm not volunteering.

Chris: It's not that they've been deliberately distorted, it's just … "Darshan" means: sight of the Master, literally. "Sahavas" means: company of the Master. And "prasad" means: gifts from the Master. And that's exactly what you were saying, Don. That is the real meaning of these words, there's no ambiguity whatsoever.

Don: Each one has a meaning. And Baba was careful about the real meaning of the words that he used, terribly [careful].

Chris: It's so interesting what you said, because now people think "darshan" is bowing down and it has nothing to do with that at all.

Participant: Could you repeat that, what they said again, what "darshan" is?

Chris: Darshan is sight of the Master. I tell you I went through a dozen – I couldn't find anybody there that even knew, because they think that prasad is an orange sweet. {Laughter abounds}

Chris: Well, "prasad" is gifts from the Master.

Laurent: Right.

Chris: Prasad is gifts from the master. A Master can use, as Baba … I've seen him many times, a banana, a this, a that …

Laurent: Sandals, a sadhra, a …

Chris: or Silence, as he says.

Participant: Nobody ever actually tells you what they mean when you arrive there.

Chris: Well, but it is all in the original, in the original writings.

Laurent: I just have to respond to that. Isn't it our responsibility to find out what things mean, not for somebody to tell us? {some talk in background amongst companions}

David Lee: Well, aren't you speaking about the image that you used, Don, initially? I kind of got lost at the thing on the train [on the third bridge]. Is that Baba's words?

¶ Don: I'm going to get back to that third bridge, you can depend on that.

David: And I was thinking that something else that is on that train is the fact that we are all eating together. That we are on the train together and that we . . .

¶ Don: We sure are.

David: And that we interact with each other.

¶ Don: Everybody sitting in this room is eating on that train.

David: *And in that sense of companionship, the inner-links that are forged, we build up a quality of being able to true the sense of what things mean, and to find the essence of the source, and to do that together.*

¶ Don: That's what companionship is.

Laurent: And each group is at a different table.

Participant: So what we are really saying is, we've got to be a bit more careful about this.

¶ Don: Exactly.

Laurent: I think Brendan.

¶ Don: Brendan?

Brendan: Yeah. I was just going to say, Don, I'd like to commute, get back to the start, really. I'm big into lost causes, but this one is really beyond me. You're never going to stop ...

¶ Don: Of course you're not. That is why Dharma decays, and [the Avatar has] got to come back. But don't we have a responsibility to make it decay less rapidly and less far?

Brendan: I agree with you absolutely, and so there's a ... so there's unquestionably a place for ...

¶ Don: Effort.

Brendan: The literal history of what went on, who said what to whom. That's what history is, when and where, who said what to whom.

¶ Don: It should be. Good history.

Brendan: So you are in a privileged position in your, "Baba said this to me."

¶ Don: Exactly.

Brendan: And that's what needs to come out.

¶ Don: I realize what a privileged position that is, and I'm trying to fulfill the responsibility of it. That's why I'm here.

Brendan: I, for one, as a short term Baba lover at least, have found it impossible if I don't try hard enough (probably haven't) to get the original copies of the *Discourses*, for example.

¶ Don: Uh-huh.

Brendan: It's a bit …

Laurent: How original is original?

Brendan: Well …

¶ Don: Deshmukh.

Participant: The five copies. The five volumes.

Participant: The three volume ones.

¶ Don: Deshmukh.

Laurent: They go before that. See. And there was …

¶ Don: That was Deshmukh.

Laurent: And before the five volumes there was the *Meher Baba Journal*, where Baba had discourses published in there. So they go back a long way.

¶ Don: Some of those discourses go back to the thirties.

Brendan: There is in the *Discourses* some degree of flexibility, because Baba didn't spell these out letter-by-letter. So you're saying that Sheriar, the single volume that is commonplace now, contains a substantial number of inaccuracies or changes or whatever. I have …

¶ Don: Quite a great many changes. {Some participant doesn't hear clearly, Don repeats}: Quite a great many changes. Yes.

Brendan: I have, half-heartedly perhaps, made some attempts to get hold of an earlier copy, an earlier edition.

¶ Don: Yes.

Brendan: An earlier version.

Don: Three sets of them have disappeared from my front room. I'm angry.

Laurent: I can give you some hints on that. If you use a computer you can go online to used book sellers, and you can request, you know, in there: *Discourses*. Many times the three-volume edition will come up and you can buy them that way.

{Several participants make comments}

Don: I've got an idea. I think it's a lollapalooza. Why don't we have a net-on-line version of the three volume work available?

Laurent: Beautiful.

Several Participants: Good idea.

Laurent: I volunteer to help that happen.

Don: [Laurent is] a shaker and a doer.

Brendan: I'm sorry. I'm at the end of the point I wanted to make. Then, since you can't stop the *bastardization* of Baba's words (if that's not an inappropriate word to use) then …

Don: It's true.

Brendan: Then, as much as you can do is put the source material out there so if anybody does want it, it can be accessed.

Don: Sure.

Brendan: And there will always be zealots, who like to say, "Hey, this is the literal word," and you know, give them their head. Can we, can we trust the [*Meher Baba*] *Journal*?

Laurent: I don't know. {others laugh} I mean, I know stories around how that's happened, see? Don may know.

Don: Most of the stories I have heard, and some of them you know from people involved, was that Elizabeth Patterson was the editor of *The Journal* for some time when the *Discourses* were originally coming out in it, and I trust Elizabeth Patterson as practically nobody else I've ever known. So Elizabeth had a big hand in it.

Laurent: There are many stories that we could talk about at another time.

Participant: So, the *Discourses*. We're saying we cannot trust them. Any other versions?

⁋ Don: No. All we are saying at this moment is they have gone through a complex editorial process. Inevitably. And this is what Purdom was aiming at when he made the famous cannon shot across the bow of the boat – That we really don't have Baba's words. We don't know what he said and what he meant, because all of his words have been, first of all, taken by secretaries, and then transcribed over and changed continually. – And that was the statement, when I made it to Baba, that horrified Baba. And he said, "Look, that may be true about some things, but I'm telling you how *God Speaks* was done and also the addresses that I give out to the public." This is Baba's answer to that important question and, boy, it is precise.

Participant: We have a group reading for *Discourses* here in the Center. We use the new translation because it's easier to get hold of. But some times we have the older ones. As Eruch and Bal Natu went to such trouble …

⁋ Don: They sure did.

Participant: It should be re-edited, then, if Chris Flagg has over-edited. Then I feel we really need an edited version put out on the internet with what the Mandali put in of the edit and not what Chris Flagg … We don't need to republish the three because …

Marion: Eruch thought it was very important during his lifetime to do that work, and I feel that what he brought to it, and Bal [Natu], should be put out for us. Sometimes you go back to the three [volume edition] version, compare it with the one [volume] version, and it is very, very different. I tend to like the one version.

Laurent: [Just because you like it] that doesn't necessarily mean it's closer to Baba.

Marion: No. So now you've brought up a dilemma for me, but I would like to know what Eruch said on it. If Eruch thought it should be edited.

⁋ Don: I think it's easily established until now what Eruch felt had to go in, and the chief thing that I'm familiar with is the number two [chapter] on the Circles [of the Avatar].

Marion: Right. OK.

⁋ Don: That was the chief thing. And then I think certainly his brother [Meherwan] will remember some of the other ones. It'd be wise while Meherwan is still alive to get his input. But this is typical of what we all feel now has got to be done as rapidly as possible: find out who did what with key words like that, before the people are gone.

Laurent: You know, I think this issue may sound strange to somebody outside of this room. You know, they may just say, "This is all wonderful. I want to read anything." But it's particularly important to us.

Marion: Yes.

Keith Ashton: Can I just put out, to the group, that I have Fred Marks' [copy of] *Discourses*?

Participant: They're a Deshmukh version. You've got them?

Keith: Yeah. And, I've never known what to do with them.

Laurent: I'll take them.

Keith: Well, I mean they're very precious for my work. I'd like to know if they would be useful to you?

Laurent: Absolutely.

⁋ Don: They are certainly valuable archive material.

Keith: Yes.

⁋ Don: They should be carefully handled, Keith. No question.

Keith: So, what?

⁋ Don: They are very rare now.

Laurent: Name your price. {laughter}. I don't think we need

to do it now.

Keith: But, anyway, I put it out to the group, that's why I mentioned it ...

Don: Um-hmm.

Participant: What is the difference between the Deshmukh [five volume *Discourses*] and the three volumes?

Laurent: Don. *Don is the difference.*

Don: I was the one responsible for that transition. And I can tell you very, very simply that I limited myself primarily to reconstructing inverted sentence structure, because he was using Indian sentence structure and it is difficult. It was difficult to transfer that in my mind into American-English. Baba knows that was the chief thing that I did.

Participant: Did he, did he check that you still got the meaning, or did he leave it to you?

Don: No, he [Deshmukh] was a perfect gentleman. Terrific gentleman. We put up with each other greatly. We could have gone into competition easily, but Baba avoided it, thank God.

Participant: I often say there's music in the [three volume] edition, which has been cut out in the editing of the [one volume Sheriar] edition.

Laurent: The color. The character.

Participant: Yes, although it's easier to read on certain levels of understanding, but what a shame. Some of that music is gone.

John: Maude Kennedy did a very beautiful work. She called it *The Unstruck Music of Meher Baba.*

Don: Yes, beautiful ... a beautiful volume she did of it.

John: I've got ... can I share ... it is from the *Discourses*?

Don: Not before lunch, John. I'm sorry. You, and the rest of my intuitions, go on after lunch.

Laurent: You've still got ... twenty-five minutes.

Don: Yeah. Uh-huh.

John: I don't know if I'm going to be alive after, until then.

¶ Don: Hmm. Really?

John: Yeah. I've been having terrible trouble with sleep for ten years.

¶ Don: Uh-huh.

John: Nothing's happened.

¶ Don: Hmm. Well, do you mind if I just tell John a couple of things that Baba told me, and one of my favorite medical friends told me? I've always been amazed at how they planted it. Just all of a sudden in the middle of nothing at all, Baba turned around the conversation Eruch, Don, Baba were having and said, "Don, if it ever happens to you that you're having trouble sleeping, Baba wants you to know that if you get four to five hours a night on an average, and you may think it's not even half of what you should be getting, Baba wants you to know that you can live indefinitely in good form on that." I always slept seven, eight hours, and so that didn't phase me at all. I thought – I'll never get down to that. But when the old ladies started dying off at the Sufi home in Fairfax, I was lucky if I got two or three a night.

Then I remembered what Baba had reassured me, and also the old family friend who was a great, early student of Carl Jung, Dr. Elizabeth Whitney, in San Francisco. Years before she had said, "Don, in my experience, I have had patients who had visions of things at a distance, and on occasion the situation would become so desperate that it would interfere with their sleep." Then in extraordinary fashion she said, "I remember one lady whose son was wounded in the desert in Libya during the American occupation [in World War II], and she could see him lying out in the desert, night after night, after night, undiscovered. And of course she couldn't sleep. So it became a terrific problem for her." And she said, "I feared for her health, over a period, and then there was a long convalescence after her son was rediscovered, and she kept seeing him. So this thing went on not for just days, but for weeks and for months."

All this time the old mother was coming to Dr. Elizabeth Whitney for help. And, she said, "I was astonished that this woman would barely get an hour, hour-and-a-half a night of sleep. But as far as her physical health was concerned, it was fine. Her only problem was *her worry about not sleeping*. That was the real problem." That absolutely opened my eyes. Excuse me for bringing that up, John. These are just two little jewels that were planted by awfully good people, one being Baba of course. Davie.

David: The four to five hours that Baba …

Don: Four to five.

Participant: Was that consecutively?

Don: Not necessarily. Total. Very often, I will wake up once every hour or two, and then in ten, fifteen minutes go back to sleep. And I just add it all up and say, "Well, I got Baba's four or five hours, even if the 3:30 am intuitions have interrupted, too. But it's good to have some of these reassurances. This is the sort of stress that we go through in modern times.

Brendan: I just … I'm sure I don't identify strongly with John. I mean certainly one phrase in my mind is, no man knows the burden in another man's heart. But I am very sure that at some point, some crippled individual, literally crippled individual, complained to Baba about their circumstance, and Baba just turned on them and said, "In this lifetime it's your job to help me under these circumstances." It is a hard deal.

Don: Yeah, well. He knows what we are capable of, and so we get on with it. Well, we've got time for one or two other just small points here.

Laurent: Yes.

Don: So, what we are supposed to start with are, sources of degradation of his words. In other words, things to be aware of where this can come in.

Laurent: We've covered a bit of that.

¶ Don: Well, you know, actually we sort of hop-scotched around here, thank God, because otherwise we've got more agenda left for this afternoon than for the three sessions we've already put in. So we are sort of doing a battle with time here, but that's sort of par for the course. The first one I've got listed here is "Misquotation of his words." That's what "little bear" here brought up a little while ago. I have so many memories and examples that I don't even dare tell him. The trouble is that if I start giving my prime examples of misquotations of Baba's words and actions, you'll all recognize the characters who did them. So I'm in a hell of a mess, still, on that one.

Laurent: It happens.

¶ Don: It happens. It happens.

Laurent: It's worse when it happens in print because that can get moved along to somebody else quoting that misquotation and then it just propagates.

¶ Don: Yes. I will tell you the circumstance, but I won't tell you what it then led to. When Baba was setting up the mechanics of the Four Language Group Sahavas in the mid 50s he invited Francis Brabazon and myself as the only Westerners. When he had the Western men come to visit him the year before, I was in the hospital with a kidney infection and couldn't come, so he took pity on me and said, "Well, Don, I'll make it up to you some way," and gave me, and Francis, this invitation to come the next year. I said to myself – Whew, I'm glad I missed the other one because I would have been one amongst thirty-five having Baba's attention, and now I was one of two outsiders to have his attention, so that was a good trade. – As soon as I got to India with Francis, Meherjee drove us up from Bombay and found we were to stay up on the [Meherabad] Hill. The meetings were to be held in old Mandali Hall down at Lower Meherabad, and when I got there in Meherjee's car, I immediately went to say hello to Baba. "I'm here," and Baba absolutely stunned me by saying, "Don, I've got something I've got to explain to you." By golly, I thought – this must be something terribly important for him to take his time right now. – People were arriving that he had invited for the first language group and they wanted to see Baba. Baba was making arrangements. He was terribly busy, right in the middle of things, and for him to say, "Look, I want to explain something to you," I thought – Well, this has to be earth shaking, probably about what's going to happen to the other quarter of humanity that doesn't get killed off in "the disaster," something of stupendous proportions. –

Baba [takes] me out around over to the little place where the Judsons live now, and he said, "Don, I want to explain to you carefully about how I've set this up." And he explains that he had a certain number of rupees in a bank account, and he decided that it was time to explain in the four major language groups whatever it was Baba wanted to say. This was especially for people who were limited on language, and he said, "I felt that I wanted to spend these rupees…" [a certain number of rupees] "…on the project." Then he said, "Of course it's Padri who has to do the mechanics of all of this. So when I had decided how many people approximately I wanted to invite, and how many rupees I had in the bank, and what Padri was going to have to do to provide living arrangements for them and food for them, it was Padri's job to tell me whether the two things would match." [The two things being] invited people and resources to care for them. Baba is a good businessman. I mean really. These things just didn't sort of happen by a miracle because he waved his magic wand. So he took, I would say, at least twenty-to-thirty minutes to explain to me how he got Padri in, and Padri asked him, "How many people?" Baba was telling me, I think it was something like 200 people total, something like that, fifty per group, or something of this sort. Don't keep me too close to the fire for this. At any rate, Padri said, "Well, Baba, that's not very much money for that many people," and Baba said, "Well, Padri, what if we do this?" Baba didn't say what he suggested to Padri, but they went back and forth, and Baba took several minutes to explain how many times Padri raised objections. Then Baba would say, "Well, can we try ..." so and so? And Padri would partially accept this, and Baba would give a little bit there. This went on, back and forth, and Baba said, "Finally, Don, I had Padri to the point where the ten thousand rupees ... he said, could handle two hundred people in this particular manner."

After Baba explained all this I thought – Well, this is the end of that, good for you, Baba, and I'm sure Padri's done a helluva job on it because he's a good practical guy."

I thought that was the end of the story. But, no, no, no. Baba didn't want me to leave yet. No, no, no. We're just really getting into the interesting part now. He didn't say that, but that was the manner in which the gestures were going. He said "Now, Don, you just cannot believe how these things do happen when *Maya* gets her hand into the middle of this," He continues, "I'm dealing with Maya all of the time." *He was always complaining about Maya, you know.*

He said, "I sent out the invitations to the fifty people in each group and of course it was by invitation. The Group Heads knew that this was, not a secret matter, but not to be discussed, because I didn't invite everybody." He said, "If everybody had heard about it, well, maybe two thousand or twenty thousand, who knows ..." and then He said, "Unfortunately, the news got out. And so first thing I knew Adi Senior was getting all sorts of phone calls, telegrams, letters, etc. from people who were saying as gently as they could, but as firmly as they could, 'I understand, Baba, that you're going to have a group, and Baba, please let me come. It's been so long since I ...' And all of these things ... " Just heart-breaking letters from all of these people flowed in. So, Baba said –Adi would read them to me and I would wonder ... well, what could I do about it, because Padri says already the budget is too tight? And I was thinking, if I even invited one or two more people into each of these groups he'd probably have a fit.

Baba didn't say it exactly that way, but these are Stevens' words for Baba. So Baba said, "Finally I went carefully over all of these requests with Adi and there were about twenty more people that I felt just had to be invited."

I've been a good worker in an oil company, and I have had to work carefully with the engineering department on budgets, and how much the engineering department can do with this many dollars, and so on. So I've been used to what we call, "an admissible overrun of budgeted money." Have you ever heard of that?

{Participants respond with body language}

❡ Don: Yeah. There we are. I said to myself – Well, that's a ten percent overrun, that's completely acceptable, and Padri certainly would accept that – even fifteen percent, if you can convince your Boss, that it's an urgent thing. But if you go over fifteen percent, that's never-never- land and you are in real trouble. So, I just thought to myself – well, by golly, Baba certainly ought to have been able to sell Padri on that. – Baba says, "So alright, I felt someway I had to get those twenty people here, but of course I have an agreement with Padri." Well, you know, the Avatar doesn't kick around his people. He has agreements with them and he goes back and renegotiates. Baba continued, "Of course, I had to get Padri in at that point," and now it's only about four or five days before this important meeting. He said,

"I had a terrible session with Padri. It was really terrible. Padri was so upset, he said – Baba, you remember, you remember this, Baba you remember that. – He kept recalling all the ways he had compromised."

Baba could be dramatic, you know, in his description. So I could just see all of this going on. The poor old Avatar … Padri getting up in a right-royal-rebellion about the whole thing. Baba said, "Finally, I said – Well, can you do this? And maybe we're going to have to get cheaper beds for them to sleep on at night, and so on – and Padri just said, 'Baba, it's too much.'"

Then Baba said, "You know what, Padri, you're very liberal on food you like. You're not lavish but you like good food. I'll tell you what I'll do. I will tell them such fascinating stories that they won't know what they are eating and you can put some cheaper food out for them to eat." {bountiful laughter}

⁋ Don: Imagine the Avatar doing something like this. I practically fell out of my chair, because Baba's sense of humor was so terrific always. Apparently it cracked up Padri, and Padri said, "Baba, I'll do it. That's all right. I'll do it." He didn't promise whether it would be cheaper food, or what would happen, in order to get all of this done. Baba said, "Don, I wanted you to know about this."

Then I thought to myself – Baba has never explained something like this to me before. Good heavenly days! And what's the vital spiritual message in this? – I think it's a wonderful story, how Baba goes about things, you know. And even the Avatar gets beset with budgets, and overruns, and so on. But there we were.

To finish off Baba tells me, "So we're alright now, Don, and I wanted to tell…" Baba had taken practically half an hour to tell this to me, when he was so busy he didn't know how he was going to get through it all, and get the people settled down in time. So, you know, I had big question marks all in my brain. I was chortling about the story, you know, but at the same time I'm thinking – Why does the Avatar take all of this time to tell me this? – I get settled and the people get settled who had been coming. The next morning (which is the first day of the meeting) we're down there in Meherabad Hall, and Baba is starting to gesture, and he is being interpreted, and the secretary is taking notes and everything is going along fine, right in gear. Then, all of a sudden, I started to hear out of the left side of my ear, here, a funny sort of a sound outside. It sort of sounded a little bit like the squeal of brakes and gravel being thrown around on the driveway. I thought – well, somebody is late, and thought no more about it. But then about two or three minutes after that, somebody beckons to Baba from way up there {Don gestures} and Baba gestures back to them, and this goes on a little bit – a little disturbance – and then finally a person comes back and gestures some more to Baba, and Baba gestures some more back to them. I don't know what this is all about, but you know, so many unexpected things happen, people wanting to see Baba for emergency reasons. These sort of things are common, so I didn't think too much about it.

    … comes lunchtime and Baba disappears. At the end of lunchtime, as I'm walking around, Baba motions to me. He wants me to come to another private session with him in the (Judson's) little cabin. He said, "Don, you cannot imagine what I just had to go through." He said, "Did you hear that noise outside as we were starting the meeting?" I said, "Yes, Baba, I wondered what it was." He said "It's five boys from …" (so and so and so and so) "… and they heard at the last minute about this sahavas, for this language group and they said, 'What are we going to do about it?' And one of them said, 'Well, the only thing we can do is get in the car and go, and the worst that can happen is that Baba will say – Go home – and so they all said, 'Oh, that's not a bad idea at all,' and they came. And of course when they came, somebody went to see what was going on. They said, 'We came to see if Baba would let us come in.'"

Then Baba said, "Here I am, Don, I just had (as I explained to you) this tremendous second crisis with Padri about building and blankets and food and so on and here are five more." Well, five more is a twenty percent overrun on that one. You know, my Boss would have, would have killed me if I had asked for anything like that. Baba said, "I couldn't tell them to go back home, Don, could I?" I said, "Well, Baba, I don't know, but I guess they're staying, aren't they?" And he said, "Well, you know, I couldn't tell them that they *could stay* before I had another session with Padri." {Laughter abounds}.

❡ Don: Can you imagine. Can you imagine. The Avatar can't say yes or no until he goes back to his chief of mechanics, you know, sitting out in the backyard. Baba went on, "So Padri came in, and we had lunch together …" and Padri said this, and Padri said that, and Padri said something else, and so on …

Excuse me, I put the wrong part of the kick line in the story. This was the time when Baba finally said to him, "Padri, I'll tell them such wonderful stories that they won't know what they are eating," and then Padri accepted it.

Isn't that absolutely incredible? But you know, this story was quoted in print later with exactly the reverse moral punch line: "The extraordinary generosity of the Avatar." So you see, I saw then why Baba spent all that time to point out to me something that he, himself, has done so carefully and under such great difficulty. And those around him completely reversed the interpretation of it. Baba was pointing out – Don, this happens. – And this is what we have to guard against.

Laurent: Didn't you wait like forty years to know why Baba told you that story?

❡ Don: It took me forty years before the answer came, yes. Then

I said – Well, this is why Baba told me that story. – And apparently I'm the only one who knows Baba's side of the matter.

Female Participant: {speaking very softly}

Don: I will comment no further on this.

Steven: But there is also another thing in there, that Baba was actually …

Don {To the woman}: … Breaks your heart. Excuse me, Steven. Go ahead.

Steven: He was actually sharing his humanity there. That it's not him saying that. Of course they can come in. But it was…

Don: But this is the way. Baba was not a dictator. He never dictated. Heavens, the tenderness with which he would await me to invite him into a part of my life. It would kill me when I realized what he had done. It's incredible. You know, I think now we have got to go on time to lunch today.

Participant: What year was that, Don, that Baba had that episode?

Don: Hmm?

Participant: What year was it?

Don: That was what? Nineteen fifty-five, fifty-six, something like that. Yeah, it was just the year after all the thirty-five Western men came over for sahavas with Baba.

Participant: {Makes a comment about the date of *Three Incredible Weeks* sahavas being in 1953}

Don: So it would be fifty-four then.

Participant: Thank you.

Don: Yeah, we did it!

4 : Sunday Afternoon

ON: MARY, COME UP AND LET'S SEE your shining face. {Don looks at Laurent holding the little tape recorder, with a little red recording light, just under Don's nose} Damn red light's buzzing again here. Shall we be silent with Baba for a moment. {pause}

Did you notice head and heart? Good stuff. Thank you, Norith. What were we talking about? Oh, now I remember what I wanted to talk about. I wanted to talk about, John are you prepared for this? Hugging?

John: There's nothing much to …

Don: To set you off? Ah, that's a good smile, John. I knew that would make him smile.

We have, I think, one of the most interesting topics on the list, communication, the expression of the Word. If you remember, I've been making quite a bit of a to-do about the grace of Baba's gestures, the manner in which he told the story when I was in New York in 1952. I was so absorbed in that, that I didn't bother to listen to a word of what the story was all about. *And that's for real.* You know, it sounds awfully nice. You like graceful people, people who know how to use their hands, and maybe their legs and arms gracefully. And Baba was really a tremendous communicator. As a matter of fact, Baba's facial expressions were a tremendous source of communication. It was one of the things you would sit and reflect on. When Baba would be using the alphabet board, in the earlier days, that was pretty mechanical. And if you didn't know anything about an alphabet board, you could get left out. But all the time Baba was communicating with his facial features, so you followed the content even if you weren't particularly listening to the translation [given by the vocalizer]. You just sort of picked up the gist of what Baba was going on about. Tremendously communicative!

Now I'd like to spend just a few minutes on part of this morning's intuition, which simply was that I had forgotten entirely yesterday to talk a little bit about how Baba communicated, really, with all of his body. You got the message [visually]. What I want to say now has the risk, should I say, of perhaps being *too intimate*. Because, after all, when you talk about the body, you know, it's sort of like the ego, and it's hard to weld that into perfection, isn't it? So, if I talk about Baba and the manner in which he used his body, that may get into territory where you might think – Did he really hug warmly, or was it a mechanical routine, or, just what were the characteristics of a Baba hug?

Regardless, this was certainly used by Baba just as he used hand gestures and the manner in which he used his features: *to communicate what he was feeling, thinking and trying to get over to you.* Actually, as the years rolled along after he dropped the body, I began to remember back to various characteristic manners in which he used the body, both to relate as well as to communicate. My review began to go much deeper especially when this publisher down in Barcelona became increasingly important to us. He wanted to do an edition of *God Speaks* in Spanish, but only after he had published a biography of Baba, which he said he wanted to be half philosophy, half his personal history. I got stuck to write that finally. It's a long story, but I finally did it. In doing it, though, I had to do a lot of homework, a lot of reflecting and remembering, but that was a useful process.

Participant: And that became *Meher Baba, The Awakener of the Age*.

⁋ Don: Yes, Meher Baba, the Awakener of the Age. This business of reflecting back, I think that's part of our homework, quite frankly. Although I've had to do a lot of remembering in the editing work and translations and so on, I had reflected very little about actual physical proximity of being with Baba. There was neither time for it, nor any particular reason for it. I think absolutely everybody is very familiar with the fact that Baba was famous for his, "Baba hugs." They were not big, tight bear hugs. I can say that. I had a lot of them, thank God. They were a great experience. But they were not rib-crackers, they weren't that sort of hugs. But they were certainly, certainly unique. So, that was one thing.

Also, Baba was a great *hand holder*. He held my hand on several occasions. The most terrific one, as far as I was concerned, and maybe the most notorious one, was when we were going back from The Barn, at Myrtle Beach, to the Old Kitchen, down the trail. And he looks around and sees me walking behind him. There were about fifteen or twenty of us in the group, and he motions to me to come up. Then he takes my right hand with his left hand and we walk along for yards, and yards, and yards. It was just a very simple, warm – *I'm here, you're there, we're one* – sort of feeling. I had no visions. I didn't fall over in a trance. I didn't yell, "Halleluya, I've had it," or anything of the sort. It was just great.

Participant: {question for Don but inaudible on recording}

Don: Nope. Just, the hands were sort of swinging up and down in between us, going along, Baba and Don sort of swaying back and forth as he stepped, and as I stepped along with him. Oh, dear me. You know, these are nice recollections. I think recollecting is part of the treasure that you have, that you need to go back and take it out of the safe, and look at it, and say, "Boy, that's a beautiful one. That is a real jewel." Yup, there they all are.

So, and on other occasions, you know, when I'd be around in a car, or something like that, well, a hand would come over and one would just sit quietly hand in hand [with Baba]. It was just so beautiful, so simple, so related. You know, these were not just the inner-links, these were outer-links as well, and it added dimension to it. I always thought of so many, many times when Baba talked to me about communicating with him about my personal life – when he said, "Now, Don, I know you've been kind and you said that you knew that I knew about your mother's death, so you didn't bother to send a telegram. But your responsibility to me, now, remember, both of us live within creation, with its limitations." *Both of us live within creation with its limitations.*

Now that was not poetry. That was *not* God saying to little Don, "I'm here and you're there." But simply God the Avatar saying to Don as a human being – We are both here on the same level – This was the thing that Eruch impressed upon me, about the beauty and the incredible experience of being with Baba in the New Life. He said, *"Don, we were companions on the same level. And you cannot imagine the beauty of being the companion of the Avatar."* When Baba talked to me of such things, there was no difference. We were there. Exactly the same level. Isn't that incredible?

So, you see, Baba said – Here we are. Yes, I know your mother has died and you didn't send me a telegram, for pity's sake. You've got to get over that. And so your responsibility is to communicate with me by the most ready physical means. Because we're both subject to the same limitations of time and space. – It was very simply put, but golly, that told me so much about being with Baba, and who Baba is. *He's not over there, he just ain't. He is right here, and he is flesh and blood with you. Right in the middle of the thing. It was a complete surprise to me.*

At any rate, in all of this, I became used to the fact that Baba was terribly, terribly, really human. He said, "I take on a lot of sanskaras to make me human so that I can participate with you,

so I don't seem somewhere else." Doesn't it make sense? It's like
– I'm the bridge, I'm not way off up there, somewhere or another, but I'm a just a bridge right here doing a straightforward
thing that's got to be done now. – It is so important to understand this and live it with the Beloved.

Time went along. Oh, incidentally, the third means of communication [that Baba used when I was present] … every once
in a while, not as often, but when I would say good-bye to Baba,
and especially if I was going to be going off back home again and
wouldn't see him for some weeks or even for months, *then he
would embrace me and he'd kiss me on the side of the neck, or the side
of the cheek, very, very tenderly. I don't think I've ever had exactly that
sort of kiss in my life, and I thought it was just wonderful.*

As I was beginning to write up all this work on Baba's life for
that editor in Barcelona, reflecting on so many of these things,
and really for he first time on the physical side of communication with the Avatar, it was a tremendous remembering and ap-
preciation and enjoying process that I had there, too. It was like
a treasure I'd never bothered to look at behind the door, to see
what was locked away there. So out it came, but it was part of
the whole process of trying to give my honest side of the biography that had to be done honestly, simply and fully.

Then I began to be a little bit more thoughtful, because I'd
been so impressed by the fact that Baba was really terribly, terribly tender. And I saw that I was no exception (I think I was a little
exception). I think I got a few more hugs, and a few more kisses,
and a few more hand holdings than many people did. I didn't
feel particularly proud of it. It was just a fact, and I enjoyed it. As
I began reflecting back on this a little bit, when groups started
coming along, and I found myself inheriting some of Murshida
Martin's old pupils, and I had a little experience already of Meher Baba personally, I thought, well, maybe I ought to give them

[some of the old Sufis] a hug.

A hug? I mean, I practically don't know that person. How do you hug somebody that you practically don't know, and what does that hug mean? I'm afraid I am this horribly honest person with myself. I look so often suspiciously at myself, too often, I'm afraid. So, it's sort of like intuition. You ought to have a little bit of faith in [them]. I sometimes didn't have much faith in myself, other than … Well, I said – if Baba can accept me, I ought to have faith to accept myself where I am. – Then I would look at myself and say – these are nice people. I practically don't know them, but they're in a group and we've got to give them some of Baba's message. And Baba very frequently would hug people as he said "good-bye" to them. Well, maybe I ought to try it. – I figured it must be a first cousin to selfless service. You know, you do it with tremendous suspicions of – where is my ego in all of this thing? – "What am I doing here?" to quote Ivy Duce.

So, what am I doing here, and how am I doing it, and where is the honesty, and what's the real meaning of all of this? And, it wasn't bad, but I ended up with a distinct feeling that I really didn't know what all of this was about, but I guess I've got to do it again next time. And then, gradually, a little bit over a period of time, I fell for this fairly early in the game. Now I hope all of you lovely people, because I think every one of you I've hugged a number of times, so now if I tell you the things that were going through my mind, maybe you'll come up and slap me, and throw me out of the window and say, "I'm never going to hug you again, Don. Now I know the inside mechanics."

Or maybe you'll hug me harder. That might be the contrary result.

At any rate, I began to realize – well, gee whiz, when I gave Marion a hug she was sort of like a ram-rod, and something must be the matter with the connection between us. – I thought she had a lovely voice because she had sung a couple of times at seminars that we had, so I had a great affection for Marion artistically, but as a human being we practically didn't know each other. Then, after a while (I don't know how many years it might have been) all of a sudden in a hug, I suddenly thought to myself – My golly, something has relaxed in Marion. I think some sort of a barrier is down between us here. – I didn't have a confidential chat with Marion about all of this. It was just something that came through the hug, and I was sort of startled by it. I enjoyed it. I thought it told me something very valuable that I appreciated, you know, because I have all of this other sense of liking Marion's voice, and her sense of humor, and things like that. Of course, every once in a while she'd get off on a bent where I'd say – Well, I like her a little bit less when she's off on that. – But nevertheless, it was a pretty good balance up to a point. So, we go along, and then all of a sudden I thought to myself – Well, geewhillikers, I think, John, is something starting to release over there, too?

{To John}: John, I did an awful lot of getting close to you and feeling you inside of myself just through our simple hugs. It's amazing how something communicates. I can't tell you what it's all about, but it made so much sense to me.

Of course, Baba knew he didn't need the hug to communicate to him what was going on, but I think he communicated something tremendously important back to the people. That's the reason for the Baba hugs. That's going, let's say, the full range of the spectrum. And then I began thinking – Now can we go into, get more psychological realms? – You know, just holding hands with Baba occasionally, just simply, warmly, unified, here I am, there you are. We're here on the same level, the same scale. It was wonderful. And the occasional kiss on the side of the cheek, or on the neck.

I don't know which is the more warm, whether the neck is or the side of he cheek. I'm beginning to have theories on these subjects, you see? If you open the door, you've got to go in and start looking around, don't you? So, I began to make explorations. Then I began to think to myself – All of this is tremendously interesting.

Then I noticed one day, one of the jolliest of the older ladies down on the Cote d'Azur – I hope she doesn't speak English, and doesn't hear this. {Don laughs} Forgive me, I'm sorry. Baba had such a sense of humor when you look at it through his eyes once in a while. He often said that, *"The reason I can bear creation is because there's so much humor in this wonderful dream ..."*

❖

Let's go now for a while to the Cote d'Azur in France, a wonderful place to spend a few moments with Baba, who also loved it. Here we are, with a very proper, very nice looking French lady in her mid-fifties, almost sixty, very well kept, as French ladies tend to be, as you well know. They keep their svelte, their chic. I always think of Madame Anthony, late into life, into her nineties. Good heavens, looked like she stepped out of a bandbox at ninety-five.

So, here we are, and here's this lady that I've known by that time for quite a few years, a pillar, and terribly interested in esotericism, loves Baba and all the very best things. One day when I gave her our usual hug, I don't know what possessed me, I pulled her a little closer and I put my ear next to her ear. Well, my soul, when she pulled back she looked at me as if an earthquake had hit. And I thought – Oh, my God, what did I do? What did I do? This is probably some kind of sign language that I don't know nothing about.

Then I thought of something or another.

{Don tries to apologize for taking so long to tell this story}: Well, excuse me, we just have to go on. I won't take too much

longer. But, have you ever heard the old 20s or 30s sort of rock –
no, that was jazz. At any rate, *Cheek to Cheek*. You know, I thought
of that, right away, and I said – Well, it wasn't cheek to cheek, it
was ear to ear, which is awful close. – And cheeks are certainly
very sensitive. I have very sensitive cheeks. They know what they
are near, and if I'm around somebody, or giving a French hug to
somebody or another, my cheek always gets involved with their
cheeks. It's natural in France. So I thought – Well, maybe it's …

Can you stand to be scientific for a few minutes? What about
nerve concentrations? I began to think about nerve concentrations. I thought to myself – Well, cheeks are in a very sensitive
part of the facial anatomy, and the ears especially so. – How
many of you remember now how many times I've said to you,
"My, your ears are cold this morning. You've been in a cold draft,
haven't you?" Well, to be perfectly honest with you, that's simply an excuse on my part to say, "I love you."

So, you see, communication can work, and Baba did… The
reason that I'm telling you this is, he was a master at this in a
very, very simple and wonderfully warming and reassuring manner. Then, I think on a bit to other things, thinking of the French
people and some of their habits. Have you ever noticed that …
I don't think there's another country in the world where greet-
ing a person, by kissing their hand, exists except in France. And
I always thought it was absolutely nuts. But did it ever occur to
you that one of the most enormously nerve-sense-charged parts
of your body is your hand? Baba holds my hand. Does that make
any sense? Isn't that the perfect means of transferring love? And
He did it so simply. There were no complications involved in it.
Kissing me on the cheek, with lips which are tremendously sensitive, of course. He never kissed me on the mouth. I guess that
might be a bit too sensitive. *Baba, forgive me for speculating. You
know how my mind works on these things. I've just got to investigate*

and think about these sorts of things.

Oh, and the other one. This one suddenly came to my mind, and this one I love most of all. I don't know why. But, have you ever seen a mother kissing the little baby's finger tips? Where is undoubtedly the most nerve sensitive part of the body? The finger tips. And what about the French girl, you know, in the movies, does this? {Don kisses his finger-tips, and blows a kiss to the group} What about it, does this all mean something to you?

Keith Ashton: Chinese medicine. The heart, it's this finger, and the pericardium, it's a little (or middle) finger.

Participant: What's the pericardium?

Keith: It's a muscle, the heart muscle, and the ... which has to do with the heart, is on those three fingers.

⁋ Don: Those three fingers. Next time I feel the great impulse, I'd better kiss those three fingers, huh?

Keith: {continues indicating fingers} Well, I doubt about that, but I doubt if that has any significance, but this is the colon, and this is the lung.

⁋ Don: {looking somewhat dubious} Oh, really?

{General background discussion}

⁋ Don: {blowing a kiss again} Perfection. It's certainly perfection.

Keith: He's revealing these three at the same time. {he demonstrates, and then continues}

But you're also taking the illusion with you. The subtle with you. The chi. The aussie, the chi. The da-nang. It goes to the cut off, so you bring in, and you let go something.

⁋ Don: Now doesn't this show Baba's providence, that we have Keith here, who can give us the real mechanics behind it? We have Norah here, who has been keeping us straight on the subconscious and things like this, and a shaker and a doer here keeping us on our toes. We're well provided for, aren't we? But

I love this business of kissing your fingers to somebody. I think I'm going to take that up. So if I greet you at the door {sound of kiss} this way at the door, you'll know exactly what it means in the future. But please forgive me if I tell you, "you've got a cold ear this morning."

Keith: {holds up his hands} Those are palmistry, of course. They say that palms are a reflection of the mind. So, I mean, when you do something as usual, your hands are usually involved in performing the action, whatever it is.

¶ Don: Yes, it's such a close connection. But the hands are so important. And Baba loved to hold a person's hands.

Keith: {continues to point to various parts of the body} The folchier, the healing part. It's called the pericardium. Pericardium. Where is it? I mean, it's there. It's where the … when you first use them it comes out in a spiral. But after a while it comes out as a straight…

¶ Don: I wonder if mine are curled or straight. I don't know.

{Everyone participates in a general free-for-all of fun and speculation}

Participant: The circle is perfection.

¶ Don: The circle is, yes. That's the way I always interpreted it around Baba. Yes, Kavita.

Kavita: I love the gesture. It's so natural, you know, It's so easy. I'd actually practice it. So when I came here and I started working here and when, instead of telling them, "Whoa, this is great!" or "You're doing a great job," I just go like that {makes sign of perfection} and I get wonderful reactions. They just love that. I've seen people respond to that more than to verbal communication.

¶ Don: Kavita, can I tell you a secret? When you smile that way it doesn't take that {sign of perfection} to pass the message. Well, we've had frankness for the day. {To Laurent}: What do you think, Buster boy?

Laurent: {jokingly} It wasn't even on the agenda.

Don: It wasn't even on the agenda? That was this morning's intuition ... this morning's feed-in. So now, shall we get back to the agenda and tackle some of these sources of corrupting the Word? Now, we've got to get our noses down to the grindstone and face the blunt realities of some of the things that have got to be addressed.

Laurent: We did quite a bit of that before lunch, also.

Don: Yes, we certainly did. We certainly did a lot on misquotation of Baba's words and selective quotation. Of course, my example of selective quotation, which always bugs me, is how many people choose one sentence of the discourse on Love, and not the two paragraphs where Baba says it takes the balance between the two, head and heart. So that, to me, is one of the most typical of selective quotations that I have ever run into. It is absolutely extraordinary how our unconscious desires, and habit patterns, get the better of us and we pick out the things that we want.

When Baba was explaining to us his definition of absolute honesty, he was saying, *"When you're going to be honest with a person, you've got the job of deciding whether you're going to tell them everything you know on the subject you're discussing, nothing that you know about it, or somewhere in-between."* And he said, "It will be rare that you decide they've got no right to what you know, or that they can't properly use anything, and that you just have to..." sort of kick 'em off and ... "be polite about it, and try not to hurt their feelings, but not say anything." Then he said, "On the other hand, it's rare when you decide that here is a person who has the right, and the capacity, to know everything I know on the subject, so you tell them all." But generally you are somewhere in-between. So he said, just to put it in a brief nutshell, "When you tell them, let's say, maybe the sixty per cent that you think they can absorb and use properly, it must be," and he said, this is what Baba means by absolute honesty, "it must be a proper balance between the positive and the negative, that you know exists. You cannot overload, that would be dishonest, the positive side just to make them happy, nor do the reverse of telling mostly things that are negative, because you're sort of annoyed with them and you want really, unconsciously, to make them unhappy. What you tell must be a properly weighted, just proportion, between the positive and the negative. This is what Baba calls absolute honesty."

As I've told you many times, this has been the most profound challenge I have ever faced in my life, because I knew at once it was for real. And I knew it was fundamentally important. Furthermore, I'd taken a vow to Baba, as a student in Sufism Re-oriented, to try in my personal life, to aspire to become able to apply such absolute honesty in my personal life. Baba allowed you all of those in-between steps, from a practical standpoint, but nevertheless, I had taken that vow and I knew it was important to me. As a consequence many, many, many, many times, constantly, not just once a day but dozens of times a day, I had quickly to pause and to reflect – What is my relationship to honesty in this thing that has come up between us (this person that I'm discussing with)? – and it is an important conversation. It goes on all of the time.

Participant: It's extraordinarily difficult, isn't it?

¶ Don: It is the biggest challenge that I've ever run into in my life, because it calls … very frequently you've got to go through all of this process of hauling yourself onto a part of the neutral plateau (as John and I call it). And then just be sure that what you are quickly trying to do, is to touch reality, and not all of your prejudices and desires, while you're doing it. When you can do that, even for a few seconds, it is extraordinary what then will happen – what then will come out. So, this has been terribly important.

So this business of trying to be honest, in selecting quotations, for instance, all of these things, very often you've got to make the judgment within two or three seconds. You can't hold it up any longer. And then, of course, you have a lot of time later on to review the decision that you made, and how you went about it, and what sort of results that it produced. And it calls for a lot of honesty again in assessing the results. You can't kid yourself.

Participant: Would it be fair to say that fifty years of practice lets you do it in two or three seconds?

Don: Well, I'm not going to try to be anything but simply honest. I don't have the faintest idea. All I can say is that I have eventually come down to the necessity to judge quickly, intuitively, way down deep inside of myself, and then try my damnedest to be honest, and assume that somewhere or another, that gradually, gradually something begins to shift inside of me so that I make better snap intuitive judgments, and that Baba is there and that he is looking on. He knows what is going on, and he is doing his best to help me with the whole process, as I'm trying to be honest and I'm trying to be sincere. That's my equation.

Laurent: But isn't this like what we talked about with Norah at lunch? The difference between a reaction, and a response?

Don: You tell them that.

Laurent: Well, yes? Norah or me?

Don: Either one. Norah says you, and you're saying Norah. So you decide between you.

Laurent: Well, it just strikes me as exactly what we were talking about at lunch. The difference between a reaction and a response. Somebody wants a *response*, and very frequently what we give them is a *reaction*. And maybe what Baba wants is an *honest response*, according to what Don has been saying, where we really weigh and consider …

⁋ Don: There's been even …

Participant: You're talking about it in relationship to spontaneity one way …

Don and Participant: Well. Uh-huh. Well.

Keith: But Don, we've really got …

⁋ Don: Some reflection. Go ahead, please, because Keith is an expert on this.

{Keith and several in the audience exchange bits of beginnings before Keith wins the floor}

Keith: Well, in fifty years … Yes, but I mean … That's absolutely right. But I mean, what I do, what I try and do is … I very rarely go onto the *neutral pathway*. I'm a great reactor. I'm doing . . . I'm fantastic at it, really.

⁋ Don: You're more brilliant at not reacting at once, any more. Go ahead.

Keith: Not quite yet. So, anyway, the thing is …

⁋ Don: He's calming down. He's on it, whether he calls it that or not. Go ahead.

Keith: What I actually want, deep down, is for my happiness and everybody else's happiness. That's what I really, really want. And that's what the neutral pathway allows me to do, if I get onto it. I can say …

⁋ Don: That's a misuse of the neutral plateau, but go ahead.

Keith: Well, I mean, this is the way I do it.

⁋ Don: Yup, you do it.

Keith: So the practice, for me, is to want the other person's happiness. So if I can tune into that, then anything can happen.

Laurent: I think, just to respond to that, if you can tune into another person's happiness, that gives you something to work with, about which part of it will make them *positively* impressed and which part will be *negative*. Because if you don't know them well enough, that's a real dilemma. If you've got to give an equal …

Keith: I'm talking about general happiness. I want the person to be happy.

Laurent: Yeah, I'm just taking this a step further with honesty, and Don's definition from Baba …

Keith: I think that will come. I think that will be accomplished. The practice of the neutral plateau is, in itself, a great feat. You know, it's an incredible thing to …

Don: It's like being consciously forgetful. It's the same thing. They're related. Terribly related.

Participant: I've been trying to be more flexible. Open up my heart, like that rather than …

Don: Holding this way.

Participant: I call them beautiful. I call these sanskaras, of which I have many millions, sanskaras, and the extraordinary thing is, to take a very small example, I didn't realize, it was a shock last week, I realized that I was holding back quite a number of complex financial problems from Baba. I was absolutely refusing to take any action on them. That was the tight fist. *So I opened my hands inside my heart and there was an extraordinary change by the end of the week.*

Don: It is incredible [what happens] when one consciously does that. Incredible.

Participant: But the alarming thing, the pride thing, that was happening to me, was both on emotional, sexual and financial … all those three, which are major fronts in my – in everybody's lives. I was really attached, so I had to consciously – that's where the work …

Don: Yes. Conscious effort. Decision.

Participant: … open up my heart.

❡ Don: And that's what [has to be done] as Baba will not act if we do not do it. That is his tact, that is his sense of ethics. He does not come in unless you invite him in, and it has to be a positive act on your part.

Participant: I think that bears repeating.

❡ Don: Yes. Baba does not come into a situation in your personal life until you invite him in. His sense of propriety is extraordinary. You have your privacy.

Participant: That's huge.

❡ Don: It is huge. I go back to Keith. Keith, because this is such an important point that you raised with happiness. We've known each other so well for so long, we can talk simply and directly on this. I felt very much as you did in relation to happiness, as being a central objective point in relation to people and how you're trying to relate to them. Until I became a teacher in the private school from which I had graduated. There I saw, just spread out in front of me, human beings, attractive, intelligent, from splendid backgrounds, and almost without exception raised by parents who above all wanted their children to be happy, and freed from worry and troubles. Great goal. And almost without exception, none of those kids could meet any sort of crisis in their own personal life, because they'd been protected from any kind of crisis by parents. This was the thing that just shocked the hell out of me, and I said – Don, you've been asleep, you've gotta wake up, you've gotta wake up. It's more complex than that.

So happiness as a goal for another person, I'm not sure I have the right to judge where they are in relation to happiness in that area of their life. I like to see happy people. I like, if I can, to do something that will, if they have a big burden, decrease that burden some way, but it has to be real. And I have to know

... I've found that people have to go through some terribly un-happy times in their lives. This is what our blessed old thing called *karma* involves us in. So there's some tit-for-tatting. And are we inadvertently going to postpone the tit-for-tatting, pos-sibly making it a bit more complicated for them, by doing that? I don't know. But I know it's a dangerous subject.

Keith: I think, it's obviously very subtle. The thing is ... what I meant was that I was correcting my vision, my wrong vision, to a correct vision. I don't mean superficial happiness, I mean, and they're enlightened ...

Don: Keith, what you are raising is not for you and me to judge, because we're not enlightened yet. But go ahead.

Keith: No, but I mean that's what I want to become. I want everybody else to do that. That's all I meant. So it's not a superfi-cial thing. I understand about sanskaras. We've been together, as you say, for a long time. On my deathbed, I know that I'll think about sanskaras (Hopefully not). They'll be around there.

Don: Somewhere, probably.

Keith: You know what I mean?

Don: I certainly do. Yes. The word happiness: I just have to leap out at it when there's any chance it could be misinterpreted. That's why I had to leap out.

Keith: Real happiness.

Don: Real happiness.

Participant: In case ... you have to be real careful if you're Irish. {jokingly}: There are special *deathbed sanskaras* if you hap-pen to be, like me, half Irish. They're not to be envied, those Irish deathbed sanskaras.

Don: Chris, what do you have?

Chris: A little digression [about] misquotations. We're here looking at it, the "Don't Worry, Be Happy" [poster]. I think it's very unfortunate, in a way, the superficial way to portray Baba, because from what I understand, that had actually been taken out of context. That was in a bigger context ...

{Several people talking}

Chris: *There you go. And with what we're talking about – that is actually – that's a terribly superficial way to view Baba. It is God, smiling and saying, "Don't worry, be happy." And your life is in hell. You feel like throwing a rock at the damned thing.*

¶ Don: But I would say, in order to be sure that you do not have the impression that all Baba people function that way – with that little discernment – come around to the Friday night or Sunday group, where we regularly go over the full thing, in which Baba puts it into context. Then he comes down [and says clearly], – If you want real happiness, if you want real love, you've got to do so and so and so and so. But that's absolutely impossible, so try doing this. – [Then he goes on in the same discourse and says] – But if you really want to start some place practical, then the greatest eater-upper of psychic energy, which you must have to make progress on the spiritual path, the greatest eater-upper of that psychic energy is worry. So if you want to start, practically, to get onto the spiritual path towards realization, and to real love, start with something practical, and master your worry pattern. – That's the whole context. That has been repeated so many times here in London, I don't know anybody who's got that one wrong.

Obviously, this is Don's version of what Baba says in a specific discourse and not Baba's words. In cases like this we do not use quotation marks, as if it was from Baba.

Chris: No, I didn't ...

¶ Don: We just wanted to give you confidence that we haven't shirked our duty to Baba's full words.

Chris: I know. It's just so funny, because it's such a good subject. It's the misquotation [through taking words out of context] ...

¶ Don: Sure. That's the temptation. Yes, Steve.

Steven Marions: In actuality, it was that [card] which drew me to Baba, with a picture of Baba's face on it. It was just, "Don't Worry, Be Happy." I was just 17. It was that which actually said, "Good Lord, here I've been … I mean, of course." {laughter and several people talking}

Laurent: I think, just to share a little briefly, I think Baba uses everything associated with him. Period.

Chris: Yes. That may be so, but it's still …

Don: That's a good flat rule, isn't it?

Laurent: He uses it, I'm not saying how.

Don: {mocking Laurent} "I'm not arguing with you…" {laughter, several people talking}

Don: {continuing} Our dog & pony act will proceed from here.

Participant: …what you just said. I just met a girl, and she told me when she first read "Don't Worry, Be Happy," she was like, "What sort of person is this? So simplistic!" And then she found out there was more to it, and that actually brought her in to Baba.

Don: And that was the door-opener. Interesting. {several people talking at once}

Participant: But it's not out of context. It's true, that this happens, but this exact clarification of naming is also really important.

Don: All right, now we're going on to number four. {To Laurent}: You got it? Shaker and doer, we go on to the next one. All right, that says that our own sanskaric coloring related to both external experiences and internal resources is one of the sources of the degradation of his words. Sanskaric coloring. Does anybody want to venture a clarification of what we mean by sanskaric coloring? This is a highly important … Matt, do you want to do something on that?

Matt: I imagine it would be our version of our sanskaras,

which would be about fear, which is the opposite of love … all the barriers we have to remove … and they can be just different variations on the theme. In the end, it's all going to be the same thing.

Don: It interests me that you bring up fear as being a central type of sanskaric coloring. So if somebody talks about what my sanskaras are going to do to color something to do with Baba, that maybe is a little distasteful, unconsciously, it will be fear within me. Marion wants to add something.

Marion Saunders: Well, I'm going to quote Mozart, because Mozart could hear the music of the spheres. He said, "When I write it down, it will be Mozartic, because it will be my coloring, what I hear." So everything looks personal. All our experiences in the whole of creation are completely unique to each individual soul. All our coloring will be completely unique.

Don : Uh-huh.

Marion: And we might group together, and even have a similar one with people with vast differences in coloring.

Don: Marion, my reaction is that I think I would just have to feel that when Mozart composed his Requiem, which as I remember was on his death bed, that he had listened to the spheres but was not clearing it with Mozart any more. Because that is unique. It is, I think, one of the most exquisite pieces of music that's ever been written. And it's almost totally non-Mozartian. This is the thing that always staggers me when I hear it. {several people talking all at once}

Marion: He didn't write all of it.

Don: He didn't what?

Laurent: He didn't finish it.

Don: Who finished it?

Marion: I can't remember who it was.

Laurent: Do we even know?

Marion: I think it was Chambolia.

Laurent: Really?

¶ Don: I did not know that story. I'm so happy to know that. Paul, what are you saying over there? (Or trying to say).

Paul Gregory: I've just got a couple of assertions. You were saying about sanskaras. I've been thinking about that. So now we, "see through a glass darkly." And the other one is Barnum-thinking, is that life, like a many colored glass ... the white radiance ...

¶ Don: Hmm. I've never heard that.

Laurent: The white radiance?

Paul: *Life, like a many colored glass, stains the white radiance of eternity.*

¶ Don: That's a beauty. I think we had better have that for Neti, Neti one of these times. Can you bring it around?

Paul: Yes. {Paul continues his train of thought}: It's an obvious thing to say, that sanskaric colorings must not have to be removed from the unconscious before we use them.

¶ Don: That's what Norah said. It is unconscious and there is no way that it could possibly be weeded out [consciously and not produce their effect]. It's going to produce it, we've got to put up with it.

Marion: But that's the beauty of it all, is it not?

¶ Don: Well, I think it's hellish, myself, but you know, you can convince me, Marion.

{much laughter and background speaking}

Laurent: There are two sides.

Marion: Oh, everything has two sides, in duality.

¶ Don: Well, I never looked at the other side of that one.

Laurent: Yes, you did.

¶ Don: Coloring upsets me. Am I wiser than I think I am? Have we got our dog and pony act on route here? {Looks over at Laurent, then laughter and several people talking}

Laurent: Remember, we talked about …

⸿ Don: You tell me. {laughter & then Laurent whispering to Don}

⸿ Don: Oh, I did say that. Let's save that for the next seminar, shall we? Boy, that will set off a few things. Marion, you're here.

Marion: If you were to ask Mani [Baba's sister] or Mehera [Baba's Beloved] the same question, the answers would be totally different and unique because of their particular sanskaras, and how they would respond to you. But Mani's would be delightful. Her coloring to her sanskaras was delightful. This is on the way to perfection. Her …

Laurent: But that's your experience of her coloring.

Marion: No, I understand her quite easily.

Laurent: No. But I mean somebody else might have quite a different experience of Mani.

Marion: But coloring is the uniqueness of the soul that comes through impressions.

⸿ Don: Now that I object to. The soul does not color.

Male Participant: Let's go back to…

Laurent: *Isn't the soul the white radiance?*

Marion: Yes, yes it is.

⸿ Don: Baba is so firm, again and again, that the soul is not acted upon, and it does not act itself. That we have got to get clear, because he says it so many times and you just know it's gotta be true.

Marion: It's not affected by the sanskaras?

⸿ Don: No. Definitely not, nor all of the pain, and so on. Norah, you wanted to add something.

Norah Moore: I just realized that I jumped in at the very beginning and we didn't define sanskaric coloring, and just need my perception, with my coloring and how I …

⸿ Don: Yes, your experience of it.

Norah: My coloring and my perception of it. {Norah had previously stated that there is no way that even the most advanced student or even Mandali can block their contribution of subconscious coloring}

¶ Don: Yes, I made a note of that. I wanted to give you a hug for that one.

Male Participant: I think it's just gotta be mentioned. I think it's been already ... the discourse on *Love*, which is always, I think, a good one to quote, that when people read the discourse on *Love*, they always forget that it is comprised of one of the other components: what is heart, is also reason. That is, you know, true love is a synthesis of those two elements, and many of us approach a particular discourse through, either being more dominated by the *head*, or more dominated by the *heart*. And in that instance, of someone being more dominated by the heart, very often the synthesis of reason is left out. In the combination of the two ... people just can't take it in. They absorb that that is also in the discourse. And that's how we are selected, because of our own sanskaric coloring. And we're all prone to it, in different places.

¶ Don: Good, good. Well said.

Keith: To follow up from that, in Buddhism, you have five Buddhas and five colors. For example, the green one is jealousy, the red one is anger, and so on and so forth. And your teacher should be able to see which segment, I presume, you're coming into this life to deal with. This, I presume, is what you mean when you say we're dealing with a particular segment [or wedge] of our mind.

¶ Don: Within a given life, what Baba made clear to me, is that we all have a pie of all of our sanskaras, but there is a particular wedge of those sanskaras which is selected to deal with [during the present lifetime], and that's what you associate with a color, and why not.

Keith: Well, I mean, it's just another way of looking at it. So you're getting the mantra of that Buddha to work with, and that depletes, that supposedly depletes the sanskaric energy, and ...

Don: Well, you're putting more technical terms together than I can absorb quickly, Keith, because you know the whole background there. But we don't have time to get me straightened out on all of the terms.

Marion: This is like a bit of criticism of the coloring, because the soul, it is pure light, but it's the way the spectrum ... every snowflake is unique, the way it disperses light is unique, so in the jigsaw puzzle every soul is unique and when its place is taken it will be totally unique. But how could we describe that uniqueness if we can't put a coloring on it?

Male Participant: {cant hear the start of the comment} ... conscious coloring, rather than unconscious.

Marion: But I think we have to love the coloring of other souls, and not ... You know, it's there.

Don: The characteristics of other souls (but let us say the sanskaric characteristics) I do not think we're obligated to love. Sometimes we've even got to help them correct [those characteristics]. That's what companionship and inner-links is about.

Laurent: This is a tricky subject.

Don: You know, we're skipping over some terribly important ground here. There's no way we can cover it all. Go ahead.

Laurent: Well, doesn't the coloring come up more tangibly, something we can really talk about, during the intuition part [of the seminar]?

Don: Well, we're coming to intuition, because I'm going to skip over number five, sources of degradation with just a quick comment, and then we are in intuition. But there is a terribly important point, it's very central. So, let's hold coloring for a little bit, if you all can, and we'll tackle it again under intuition.

But now I'll read to you what point five under sources of degradation is: "Failure to attribute sources of material used in later books." This to me is a cardinal negligence of the rights of the person for whom you are writing, [the reader]. They have a right to know where the material came from, from what source, because one of the most important things is that the different sources have varying degrees of reliability. This is the key.

So, if such-and-such's name is penned to this, and I happened to have read or happened to have known the guy, and say, "Well, he was a terrific stinker! He didn't know what he was talking about half the time." {Don pauses thoughtfully and then continues}: I don't talk like that about most things, but you get the idea.

Then, you just say to yourself – That particular material, I'll put a big question mark. Or maybe I won't even read it, because I have so little faith in that particular person.

Then another [book] is attributed to another person, and that individual, you know, is very careful about what he put down, and really ruled himself with an iron fist, looking for the original source, and interpreting it correctly with careful words. So you say, "Yea, that attribution is good, and I'm going to really pay very careful attention there." Proper attribution is one of the most fundamental responsibilities that a writer has to his audience. End of story.

Laurent: Well, can I just add a tiny piece to that? We could learn a lot from Islam about this, because every piece of the *Hadith* (which is the stories about the life of Mohammed and what he said) gives very carefully something like, "Meher Baba said to Don, & Don said to Bruce, & Bruce said to Laurent, that Baba said …", and they give all that, every time they quote anything.

May Allah bless him and grant him peace.

⁋ Don: Yes, they're meticulous.

Laurent: They're meticulous, and people have their favorite lines [of transmission] and people whom they trust, and other people say, "Ah, I don't believe that."

⁋ Don: That's right.

Male Participant: I think it's more, which leads to a wonderful suggestion. Getting the whole of the *Discourses* onto the Internet. The whole of the group, your green volume edition. What would we all say about getting our favorite Baba quotations also onto the Internet?

Female Participant: With attributes.

Male Participant: With attributions.

⁋ Don: Well, you know, this I think is another wonderful project that needs doing. I suppose, eventually, it's this old business, there are so many things that should be thought of, and done, that priorities will have to be set up. But I feel that the *Discourses*, themselves, are one of the first that serious thought should be given to. Then, maybe there's a little committee of two, or three, or four persons who are constituted to worry about these things, and discuss them, and discuss them with other people, and other groups, and find out what the next one should be to go onto the Internet. But it's a big project and an awful lot of responsibility to other people involved.

Male Participant: Baba's words as a screen saver.

⁋ Don: Baba's words as … {Don is obviously not clear about what this means}

Male Participant: Baba's words as a screen saver. {laughter}

Female Participant: People will have big things going across the screen and …

Male Participant: Dinosaurs.

Don {trying to assert control again}: You know, probably our old friend here, Laurent, who's a great computer and language expert, is going to have to educate me on this, but I have never heard about "screen savers."

Laurent: You don't use one. Don doesn't have a screen saver.

¶ Don: Oh, well, that explains it. I don't have it so that's why I don't know what you're talking about.

{Laughter and several people speaking}

¶ Don: Well, you see, I've got to be educated.

Laurent: I'll show you later.

¶ Don: The shaker and the doer is going to shake a little bit more and we'll do it.

John: That's two of us. I don't know what a screen saver is, either.

¶ Don: That's OK. When I find out I'll let you know, John. We'll learn it together.

All right, shall we go into *Baba's gift of intuition*? 'Cause this is enormously important. Could I just simply say, flatly, and bluntly, I would go right back to that first thing, before we start. That the major use of intuition for us, I feel, is *to fill out Baba's words*. For instance, as you read through *God Speaks*, finally when you get down to it you find that what Baba has put there is simply the skeletal, the bare bones, material for an enormous panorama of creation and God's Will within it. Many, many, times in later years in editing various different translations of Baba's works, I have said to myself – *How many times have I read that sentence, and never realized what it implied?* – So the penny finally drops, and I see a rich new panorama of meaning I had never suspected to be there. To me, the fact that *God Speaks* comes in the incarnation when the Avatar gives us his *Avataric gift of intuition*, says to me, "These two things have got to be linked up." I am absolutely dead convinced now that intuition is Baba's intended tool for really getting deeply into the meaning and the value of *God Speaks*. This, to me, is the important marriage that's got to go on, and a lot of people have got to take it terribly seriously.

I've got to be honest with you, and the first thing I've got to say is something in the form of an introduction to the entire subject of Baba's gift to humanity of intuition. I'd been talking about the gift of intuition for at least thirty, maybe forty years, when I was due to arrive in Seattle, for a short *God Speaks* seminar. There is an awfully nice guy there, named Lance Bonnington, who has always been around when I've been there in the past. Frequently, he picked me up at the airport and carried me around here and there.

This time, after the Seattle seminar, he carried me on down to Oregon. At some point, shortly after my arrival in Seattle, I was telling him that one of the things we would take up during the seminar was the role of intuition in relation to *God Speaks*. I mentioned, of course, that this was very important, being Baba's gift to humanity. Lance said, "Don, you know, we've known each other a long time, and I enjoy you and you enjoy me, I think, and we're honest with each other. We've spent a lot of time … and you know me well enough to know that I've tried to do a good job, first of all, to read everything of Baba that I could lay my hands on. Secondly, I've tried to get to know as many of the Mandali (who are still living) as possible, and so, I've collected, I think really, a very … almost a professional background of available material. But you are the only one that I have ever heard use this expression: *'Baba's Avataric gift of intuition to humanity.'*"

I stared at Lance absolutely thunderstruck. Really, I couldn't have been more surprised, nor more shocked. So I said, "Well for pity's sake, that astonishes me, because, yes, I know all the work you've put into this background of doing your homework. And do you mean to say that you have never read anything, nor heard anybody talk of Baba's Avataric gift to humanity being intuition, just as Jesus Christ's Avataric gift to humanity was love?

And, I think also, that undoubtedly people who heard that part heard Baba say another one, I think it was Mohammed, gave a third example of Avataric gift, but 'so and so' I could never remember. And because 'so an so' I could never remember, it became quite a broo-ha-ha."

Lance said, "I never heard that, Don, I never heard anybody mention it." Then I said completely astonished, to Lance, "Well, frankly, I'd just assumed all of this time that this was such a tremendously important part of Baba's function, as an Avatar in creation this time, that everybody knew this, and that it was noted down in all the principal books. It's got to be in [*The God-Man* by Charles] Purdom, good heavens. It ought to be in some of Bal Natu's work, and Bhau's." Lance insisted, "I've never seen it anywhere," to which I replied, "Well, you really, really have floored me."

Then I began checking with some of the people that I've always assumed, back in India, must have been in on it. They all said exactly the same thing. I don't know how many times, to how many people, I said, "But this is incredible, because I was sitting in Mandali Hall not once, but twice, when Baba brought up this particular subject, and I remember him so clearly going on to say that *intuition will be used not only in creative areas but also importantly in highly technical areas*. It will become the primary tool, for instance, in the disciplines of sciences, engineering and so on."

Completely amazed I said – This is so earth shaking, how can people have forgotten this? But person after person said to me, "Don, this is the first time I've ever heard of that." All this was so real, you know. Sometimes, but very rarely, I have to admit that, someway or another, Baba will get a message to me that is so terribly important and real that I assume Baba had to have said it. But this one has so much physically verifiable background. The first time I heard it, I remember going back to the group, I think it was in San Francisco, and saying, "Well, boy, this is important. Baba says his gift is ..." so and so, and so and so. And His examples were, "Christ gave love and ..." when I got to, "the third one that he gave was ... ah, ah, ah, ah ... Oh, God, I've forgotten what the third one was," I'd have to say.

Of course I was terribly embarrassed, and they'd say, "Didn't you make any notes on such an important thing?" And I said, "No, I'm not a note taker." And so they said, "Well, for pity's sake, ask Baba, the next time, because we ought to know the third example." So it was a real broo-ha-ha on this one. And all this you don't make up in your mind, or have a dream, and then, it's all forgotten when you come out of the dream. This was common tinder in that particular group.

So the next time that I went back, Baba didn't talk about it, and I didn't think to ask, either. But another time when I went back, he brought up the same thing in Mandali Hall again. And there was the third example, and I thought, "Oh God, that's so obvious. I'll remember it this time." No notes, again, of course. So I go back and I tell the group, 'Well, Baba said it again and Baba's gift, of course, is intuition and Jesus Christ's gift is love, and, uh-uh, oh, no, I've forgotten it again."

You know, you don't imagine situations like that. *They're just too damn real in illusion.* And the other part of all that was, I had this close friend, Joe Henderson, who is now "Mr. Jung of America." He's an important psychologist, one of my closest friends, and I was telling him all about these Avataric gifts. He knew about my relationship with Baba, and so he listened very sympathetically, and he said at one point, "You know, Don, that's very interesting, because that was part of my thesis [as a student]. I did some research work on the usage of the word 'love' before the time of Jesus Christ and afterward. It was striking to

me, the difference in the context of the word 'love' before Jesus
Christ and after." Then Joe went on. "What Baba said about love
being the Avataric gift of Jesus Christ makes great sense to me
chronologically."

I just don't make up conversations like that. I'm just not that
… even my dreams are not that imaginative. So there we are.
These things are indelible. Now you have sitting before you apparently the only living person who heard Baba say, "My Avataric gift to humanity is that of intuition." Now I have to make
my confession to you. So let's go on from there.

Chris: I heard Kitty talk about that.

Don: You heard Kitty …

Chris: Yeah, when I …

Don: Well, Kitty is dead. And apparently she didn't get the
word around to too many people. And apparently she didn't get
it down in writing.

Laurent: But it's a good confirmation.

Don: Um-hum. I'm glad, yes, historically, that you said that.
{several people talk}

Participant: It may be in her book. {more group talking in the
background}

Don: Well, if you find it in the writings of any of the close
ones to Baba, please let us know. Because I feel dreadfully ex-
posed on this dreadfully important subject. An Avataric gift of
intuition is not something you mess around with, it's important.
So, are you going to sign a written statement on that?

Chris: I don't mind. I feel very clear in my …

Don: Yes, I think you should do it.

Laurent: Can you hold that [microphone] near Chris and have
him say that again? {laughter, several people talk}

Chris: Well, I can't remember the basis …

Laurent: No, but the gist.

In *Discourses*: The Avatar, Meher Baba, makes a similar statement, about the "transition from reason to intuition …" See the paragraph starting, "Avataric periods are like the spring-tide of creation …" — Laurent

Chris: The gist was exactly that. That Baba was ushering in the age of intuition. These are, as I said – this is not verbatim – the gist of it. Baba's Avataric advent was to usher in the age of intuition. Which is a transition form the age of "reason."

⁋ Don: And there was Kitty, who was speaking about this.

Chris: Yes, but it was in … it was within the context of conversation. It wasn't Kitty making a statement. It was in the context of a conversation that I'd been having with her.

⁋ Don: Well, good. That's fine.

Male Participant: Which is far, way far better.

⁋ Don: Well, I'll take it either way, frankly. Because when Kitty says it, well, you know, Kitty was not … She was a grand person, and she just didn't make things up out of whole cloth. She was completely straight and honest. All right, so that's the first part of it. Now: intuition as a resource for inner contacts with Baba – resources of intuition. Laurent, you're a specialist on that.

Laurent: Well, you're going to do [part] one [as listed on the outline], and I'm going to do two, right?

⁋ Don: You're going to do intuition, a resource for extension of Baba's words.

Laurent: Yes, right.

⁋ Don: So I'm going to trade punches with you on [intuition as a] resource for inner contact with Baba. I remember my immediate reaction when I heard Baba say this, was – Thank God. Now, for the first time, when the Avatar drops his body, we will be able to keep in touch with him, those of us left behind. – That was my instinctive reaction, that intuitively, internally, he had provided the means for us to stay in touch. That is, in itself, a dangerous assumption, because that means I have to use some sort of psychic capacities in order to do that. I have to flush this [inner contact] out with something that has been for me a long, tough anatomical hypothesis of what the human being looks like. For me, it [can be represented with a] very simplified pattern. It's not a skeleton, as a matter of fact. Here, at the top, {Don raises his hand over the top of his head} I've got the drop- soul-Avatar-God. They are all the same thing for me. That is the top of any human being. And then, right underneath that, is a body, which is labeled "mental body." Underneath that is another one labeled "subtle body," and underneath that one is a nice big one called "gross body," physical body.

Then, in my mind, connecting all of these straight down, is something that I call the *vertical line of communication*. Now this is all Stevens' terminology for himself. This is how I put the [spiritual] anatomy together. There is something that communicates, or can communicate, how it all happens. What the manner [of communication] is, and what the substance [that transmits the communication] is, I would not pretend to know, but I'm sure it's there somewhere, and sometime science is going to find out that it is there and how it works.

This is going to be an extraordinarily exciting research job, when we've got the tools sensitive enough to do it, because all this happens within creation. Anything that goes from the mental body to the subtle has to be within the upper confines of creation, and it will be "sensible," and able to be sensed.

To go back [to the model of the total human being], here I've got in mind this vertical line of communication from drop-soul, Baba, God, down to the mental body. The mental body is where, amongst other things, the sanskaras are stored. We've got to get back to that one. Don't let me forget it.

Remember, Baba went through something after the New Life which he called *Manonash*, the destruction of the mind. When we got his flyer that he put out, and Ghani sent out, or rather, Adi Irani sent it out to us, it sort of horrified me, all this business of the destruction of the mind. I was thinking – What under the sun is [Baba] doing? What's going to happen to my mind one day? I like my mind. I'm friends with it. –

{Returning to the subject of the model of the total human being}: From the mental body, one goes on down to the subtle body. Here we have got, let's say, things that are more dense: emotions, and we start to pick up the energy drive, which then goes down to the physical body, and powers our physical actions.

In all of this, I've gradually come to some conclusions. Excuse me, but now I'm going to lay out a sheer Stevens' anatomy concept developed by Stevens for Stevens' own explanations to himself about how things work. It is nothing I want to convince you about. Please don't take it that way. I'm just being honest with you, the way this thing gets set up for me. And also, let's be frank, this gets deeply involved in intuition.

To put the matter simply, I've become convinced that the motor reflexes for the physical functioning of our body come from our natural sanskaras stored in our mental body. Everything that I've read and know from Baba convinces me, that's the way our body functions. We don't have to will our heart to beat, we don't have to will our gastric juices to do this, and that, and the other thing. These, to me, are sanskaric residues remaining from the terribly primitive days of the drop-soul, and its appended bodies. They're stored, we know, these sanskaras. Baba says the natural ones start long before human volition starts to occur, they are persistent. And he tells us that they are almost impossible to eradicate. And thank God they are because, I'm convinced, if we did eradicate them, we'd stop our bodily functions and we'd die.

Here we are then, a terribly important function going through this vertical line of communication from the mental body, picking up energy in the subtle body, coming down and running our bodily functions. To me, it's a beautiful thing.

All right, but what happens then if there is some sort of a defect, or a breakage, or an injury, that occurs in this vertical line of communication between the bodies and the drop soul? Well, if it's a break, or an injury below the mental body, it means we get into some problems physically, don't we? That is, if my hypothesis is correct, that our bodily functions depend on the natural sanskaras stored in the mental body.

To me, this becomes terribly important when one starts to get into external psychic communication. Now, I'm going to have some awful mad people around the world, I know, when what I'm saying now hits a few more geographic areas, because there are just an awful lot of people who have psychic communications. *But to me the great, great, really great tragedy that can happen is that this may inevitably involve a break in this vertical line of communication, or cause somewhere a distortion, or an insertion into it which risks damage.* Then, if it is repeated constantly, the risk becomes greater and greater.

All this takes me back to conversations I had with Stuart Edward White, who was in my opinion America's greatest writer on esoteric

For more information see *The Unobstructed Universe,* by S.E. White.

subjects. He was one of the greatest wild-western story writers of all time. He was a boon-companion of President Teddy Roosevelt, and they went together on expeditions hither and yon. He was a man of no mean cultural background, and born into a very, very wealthy family.

His wife, Betty, they found out, was a natural psychic, and they handled it very, very delicately. But he was the one – one of the ones – who pointed out to me *that people who are continually involved in psychic contacts, gradually start having very noticeable problems.* Very often they start to get a little pale in their coloring, they get a little bit heavy and puffy, and so on. Then often they become a little bit absent, and so on, and they can even start developing functioning problems in their physical body, which are almost impossible to trace down. Sometimes you can't even find any particular disease that's involved, or microbe, or infection, or anything of the sort.

All this sounds, to me, just dangerously, dangerously like interference with the vertical line of communication. Now I know this may sound like sort of a detour, because this is not the sort of thing that I have discussed with many people. I certainly never sat around and tried to explain this to Baba-people with whom I'm close. But this has been my inescapable conclusion, particularly over recent years, and I feel now that this is one of the things (for better or worse) that I just have to lay on the table. I know clearly that it is something that has enough possibility of being true to compel us to consider it seriously. Also, I sit often now and I remember, and remember, and remember Baba saying so clearly that *the Avatar and the Perfect Masters almost never give psychic occurrences, happenings, experiences to their devotees, but far prefer to leave them under the veil.*

This just made tremendous sense to me. It said – There's too much at risk there – So they take a safe route, and I think the safer route is the *intuitive* route. That's why I bring it up here, in relation to the gift of intuition, and also why I think it's so terribly important. Now, have I scared the life out of everybody? Have I let a phantom loose around here, which is really going to shock everybody? I hope not.

Male Participant: Well, we're all veiled, Don, so … {laughter}

Don: We've got a really select crowd for this. {laughter and background talking} They're all led on the straight and narrow. Marion.

Marion: Is the path of love, well, closed, with all of the intuition closed down as well? I mean, if Jesus brought love, and then the path of love closes, and Baba re-introduces it, or it's going to close in a few hundred years, so where will the intuition go as well? Have you thought on that?

¶ Don: Well, I certainly can't say that Baba said anything on those two occasions in Mandali Hall, which I know I saw and heard, about anything to do with intuition being anything other than a permanent gift. When he says that all universities, the technical sciences and so on will all come to depend first of all, on intuition ... And he added this each time, this was important: "But this does not mean that heads and intellect and reasoning will be discarded. They are absolutely necessary to work hand and hand with intuition as a checking mechanism." And when he says, "checking mechanism," this meant that therefore intuition can have some flaws in its operation, and that's what we've got to look at.

There's an enormously important project going on, I think, that started out actually in Atlanta, moved up to Myrtle Beach, and now is in much further stages. Laurent is a good authority on that, so I'm going to let him tell you a bit about what's going on there.

Laurent: Sure.

Marion: Can I just finish off? Anyway ...

¶ Don: Baba implied, in other words, that [the Avataric gift of intuition] goes on for centuries, and centuries, and centuries.

Marion: The other thing that was Baba's gift to us this time was the *New Life*. And that, he said, would live forever.

¶ Don: Bless your heart. Bless your heart, Marion. {then both talk for a bit}

Marion: The relationship with God has changed from *God-almighty in heaven* to *God our companion*.

Laurent: Well, I think of that as much more than a gift.

❡ Don: That is blazing a trail, and the trail has been blazed, and it's going to stay there.

Laurent: *It's almost like a new world.*

❡ Don: Remember, he said that it will be there even if there is no human being left to live it. That one we know stays.

Marion: But did he say the path where [the gate of love] would be open, would eventually narrow down?

Laurent: I think that we are really in danger of misunderstanding that. I get really antsy when I hear that, because I think it could easily be misunderstood.

❡ Don: He's a romanticist at heart, so that really rubs him the wrong way.

Laurent: Could I just say one word about it?

❡ Don: Why don't you say three words?

Laurent: Three words. Hmm. My understanding of it (which is a tiny little dim understanding) is that the collective experience of humanity, of Meher Baba's love, will be different in the future. *Not that people can't approach God through love.* And if it gets misunderstood, I would be really sad.

❡ Don: I hope today that we're going to get onto the Three Bridges, but we're going to have to go fast on it. {To Laurent}: You tell them about the intuition.

Laurent: All right. So Don collected a bunch of people together, especially Neal Lundgren and Tom Hickey in America, to bring together choice authors to write about intuition, various different subjects on intuition. And the writing has been done, it's a few steps away from publication. It could even be published this year, God willing.

❡ Don: Kendra Crossen being one [author].

Participant: How long is the book?

Laurent: Like, number of pages?

Participant: Yes.

Laurent: Two hundred, maybe.

Don: Three hundred, maybe. Now, you're going to get not only that, but also intuition as a resource for Baba's words, the pros and cons.

Laurent: I know. I've been thinking about this. Can you phrase it as a question that I could respond to?

Don: Yes. What does intuition have to do with Baba's words? Does it have any importance?

Laurent: It does to me.

Don: All right. You tell us why it's important to you, then.

Laurent: For example, when I was writing … I'm just going to tell this story because I think it does serve us here. When I was writing on intuition, Don had chosen the subject on intuition that I should write about with Jack Small. I was stuck on one point, which was this idea that Baba gives in the *Discourses* about "inborn wisdom." In other words, we have intuition from inborn wisdom, or what Don calls "inherited wisdom," where we know something based on our past experiences, from past lives, that carries over to the present. That's different, apparently, than intuition that comes from the drop-soul, Avatar, God, down to us as Baba trying to get something over to us. It's also different from a third type of intuition, which we haven't even talked about yet.

Don: Which many people would refuse to call intuition, but go ahead.

Laurent: We'll save that one, right? Keep them on the edge of their seats. And I was stuck, trying to understand – what the heck is inborn wisdom? It's just words, right? *It's great words from Baba*, and I'm reading it over and over again, and it's nice to think that we have inborn wisdom that we carry over, but I really didn't know what he meant.

Don: And He also uses the words, "stored wisdom."

Laurent: Yes. And it gets even more complicated when you talk to Don about it, because then he brings up all sorts of issues that I've never even considered before. And I was just really stuck. Where does this wisdom, or inherited wisdom, or intuition from inborn wisdom or … where does it come from and where does it get stored? I don't understand anything about that.

So, I was reading Dan Ladinsky's book, the new one, *Love Poems from God*, and I was totally opened up, and totally moved, by what he had done with the words of all those different saints and masters.

Don: He's the best-selling Hafiz interpreter.

Laurent: He's amazing. He's an amazing man.

Don: He's great. He's a Baba lover. Deep.

Laurent: [I was actually on an airplane and] I was reading and reading it, and I saw that the plane that I was on was about to land, so I immediately put my book away, put my seat belt on because it can be kind of rough. As soon as the plane touched down on the tarmac, I just got [an intuitive] flash about inherited wisdom, which was very strange, but that's how [intuition] goes.

Don: Sure does, it's strange.

Laurent: The last thing on my mind was inherited wisdom, because I was deeply moved by what I had just read – Mirabai, or St. Francis or whatever – And it was as if Baba had parted the curtain about that one subject of inherited wisdom, shown it to me and then it was closed again, and I was just left with it. I'm going – Wow, now I get it. –And as soon as I got off the plane, I wrote it up, and it's in [our] chapter for the book.

Don: Tell them what the chapter says in three words.

Laurent: Well, it basically says there are three sources of intuition. One of these is, as Don said, "drop soul, Avatar, God." The second one is "inherited wisdom" in the mental body, and the third one is "intuition from sanskaras."

Female Participant: In the present life, or from the past lives?

Laurent: In the present life. *Intuition from sanskaras*. Which I rebelled against in another way, but that's a-whole-nother story. I don't know that Baba says anything about intuition from sanskaras, but Stevens does, & we went around & around about that.

Don: He can't get his chapter into the book unless he gets by me, and that's the trouble.

Laurent: *Yes, that's the trouble*. But anyway, there are all these issues, and for me, that one story was intuition extending, for me personally, what Baba had stated in the *Discourses* about inherited wisdom. Because he just gave a little [in *Discourses*]. He said that's a source of intuition, but he doesn't go on to explain it.

Don: A source. An important source. He emphasized ...

Laurent: But he doesn't then go into an explanation ...

Don: No. He sure doesn't.

Laurent: He leaves it right there. A little stub, and then you have to take that stub and extract it. That's it.

Don: Your three little words? You're not going to talk about sanskaric intuition?

Laurent: I did already.

Don: You did?

Laurent: You missed it.

Don: Oh, I see. I see. Boy, Don, you slept by that one fast.

Female Participant: Can I ask about sanskaric sources of intuition?

Laurent: Well, this is where you get into big trouble, right? Especially with Stevens, because you've got to deal with that. Where do sanskaras come from, where are they stored, and how do they influence an intuition from drop-soul-Avatar-God. How do they influence intuition from inherited wisdom, or what if the intuition itself is only from sanskaras? And then where do sanskaras come from? Are they from the present life, the past lives, or what? It's a huge number of issues.

¶ Don: I see Bruce sitting back in the corner, looking contemplative and wise, and smiling and saying – Boy, I've been through this for thirty years now. – {laughter} He's an expert on sanskaras. Just to put it terribly simply, I'm afraid I have to define an intuition, for myself, as something which suddenly appears in the conscious mind, ready formed, and it is usually fairly definitive and clear. But then I back up and say – Well, what sort of things can come like that, clearly, suddenly, from nowhere? You haven't been thinking about it, and so on. – And then I remember how many, many times I have had sudden clarities, and impulsions to do things.

Many times I've talked with friends who have had such experiences, and they all say, "I had an intuition suddenly to do…" so and so, and so and so, and then from that point on the story usually works out in one of two directions. Either it worked out terrifically, it was a wonderful intuition, it produced wonderful results – that's one fork of the road – or there is the other situation where the person says, "It just all seemed so great to me, and I got all excited about it, and I pitched in, but it turned out terrible. It was a lousy intuition."

In other words, intuitions can sometimes work well, and sometimes they can work poorly. So, I had to say to myself, – Well, I know enough about my own sudden, clear impulsions in a given direction to know that I have had gradually (and I'm trying to be honest with myself) I've gradually had to say to myself – Oh, boy, that one came from a deep seated desire pattern. – Because it's something I wanted, I christened it, "sanskara."

It has all of the characteristics of a sanskara, but all of a sudden it's there, and it just seems so necessary and it's so crystal clear, and so you trust it. But I just have to be honest with myself. I've known a few too many of those in my lifetime, which stretches quite a while now, so I have to conclude that certainly this came from sanskaric impulsion, a desire background.

Years of observation and reflection have forced me to say, "Well, this [sanskaric energy] is also a resource for an energy pattern to come out into the conscious mind, terribly clearly, and very, very strongly. And if my definition for an intuition is that it is something that arises from seemingly nowhere, then clearly I've got to include sanskaric sources for intuitions as well. For me there are three levels of intuitive resource:

1. Drop-soul, God and Avatar. And those are reliable and, I think, very, very quiet ones usually.

2. Then at a second level we've got the inherited, or stored wisdom. Baba says that when you drop your physical body and go over to the astral side, you go though a process which is terribly strong emotionally, and during that process it is almost as if the original energies (and so on) of those experiences are burnt to a crisp. I've come to the conclusion that when one goes on the spiritual path, that process is under the supervision of a Spiritual Master, and it's for good. And so when you go through it, you go through it honestly. Then the residue is stored as a pretty pure type of experience, which is pretty dependable. But the residue is stored, Baba says it is stored. I always think of it as the sanskaric ash of previous lives, when you're on the path. So, that's the second one.

3. I also just know, though, way down deep in my bones, that I've also got an awful lot of stored energy in my mental body, which is just plain sanskaric habit and desires. Then, all of a sudden, here's a situation that comes up and I say, "Oh, golly, I've got

to do so and so and I just feel inspired to do thus and such." Maybe it turns out terrible, and I find I'm terribly disappointed and really upset about it, which is a sure sign that there was a lot of desire pattern mixed up in it. And so, that to me is the third source.

{To Laurent}: Yes, sir.

Laurent: I have to say what I said to you when you brought this up to me originally, because I really struggled with this sanskaric-intuition a lot. For me, it is very, very important not to judge on the surface the intuition, because the surface level examination can be extremely misleading.

¶ Don: It sure can be.

Laurent: We know from Baba's own life, that he would give direct instructions verbally to a disciple, and the results, *on a worldly surface level*, would look disastrous, like Ghani sweeping out his apothecary (or his clinic), and then it gets shut down, things like this. But there is a deeper level of results that has to really be tuned into, and that can be almost impossible to do alone. Sometimes it requires other people who you're close to, to help get some perspective around the results. And that's where the companions come in, I think.

Male Participant: After a passage of time, because these things take some digesting.

John: Well, when does the alchemy of forcing to reflect come into these very deep sanskaric knots, because you've just said, realistically, you've got something like intuition, and it's a very, very fierce desire that has come up as an intuition at the drop of a hat. We all know that. We all know that from our personal experience.

¶ Don: John, I'll attempt a fairly short answer (I hope a fairly precise answer) to what you raise, to what happens eventually to these sanskaric intuitions. I think here we get to the point that Baba certainly does say: that sanskaras are stored as psychic energy knots. All right. And that's what actually motivates. When you get into a situation in life, an ambience, which wakes up this sanskara, it's like a coded situation, and a similarly coded energy is stored inside of yourself. So the coded energy [ambiance] wakes up the similarly coded sanskara when the ambient situation is right for it. In the process of its coming to awakening, the sanskaric energy becomes active. It is no longer stored in an inactive form.

I have noticed that if there is something which occurs before that energy is plunged into concrete action, and which allows the energy to be left alive but unrelated to an external situation, then it acts just like any other sort of energy. *It's like a cloud, and part of it starts dissipating and it floats off and disintegrates. I've actually had what were almost waking visions of how this has occurred. When an energetic pattern is awakened, and it's stopped in its tracks, a certain amount of the energy dissipates before it is then captivated and wrapped into a physical action, or a decisive action.*

I call to your own attention something I'm sure you will all recognize. If you have been able to stop yourself in an important and rather explosive situation, and stop and say, –Heavens, this is so important, it's so desperately vital in my life, that I've got to reflect on it a bit. – So you reflect, and perhaps you say, – Well, yes, it's complex, but I've just finally got to take a chance, – so you decide on a course of action and march in.

But when you have stopped and reflected some moments, you find that what you do in that instance is a lot less explosive and a lot more controlled than other situations where you immediately leaped into action. You have a much greater sense of – you are there – and a certain amount of control is being exercised, and you feel a great deal more at peace within yourself, even if it ends up as a disaster.

All this says to me that an important fraction of the sanskaric energy has been dissipated. I think this is essentially the technique that the Avatar uses with us, especially in the provisional ego. The provisional ego is a *stop-pattern*: "What does the Master want me to do?" That simple question posed to oneself is an important "stop" action. When something is important enough to get you to stop before you leap into action, some of the pressure dissipates. And when that is done a sufficient number of times, a very important component of the energy is definitively dissipated. I simply call this the, "deenergizing of the sanskara."

Laurent: Is it connected with sublimation?

Don: I think sublimation is deeply involved in this. In effective sublimation you're finding something which becomes a provisional ego for you. Some other value, some other good around you, and you focus your attention on that. And it begins to have a value which is more important than a related desire pattern you have. This is true sublimation and it's a natural process.

Female Participant: I'd like to go back to something that occurred to me while you were speaking about intuition. You were talking about good and bad ones. And this might be helpful to some people: *What started us on this path was a whim, and to me I would feel intuition is when I break through to that whim. The whim is to know God, and intuition is something that helps me get nearer that goal.*

In another situation, I'm hungry and I want to go and eat, and I do. But if the thing that's come through to me very clearly is something that is moving me nearer to that whim, of – who am I – then I would call that intuition, on any level.

Don: Many people do insist on calling intuition only that sort of impulse that comes through that you find ends up carrying you to that end. Many people say everything else is not intuition. But it depends on how you define intuition. I feel that's a very laudable definition of intuition, but I just don't think it covers the whole subject.

Laurent: It is nicely said, also.

Female Participant: If a psychic were to say, "Ah, I see your mother, and you should do this, and you should go to this interview." That's a psychic experience. It isn't necessarily related to the whim of finding – who I am – is it?

Laurent: I think that [psychic experience] is what Don would call "breaking the vertical line of command," isn't it?

Don: Yes, and that is dangerous.

Laurent: And people who rely on that get in trouble.

Female Participant: When it moves us forward to inner teaching, I suppose, the end result may bring us to the end of the whim. I have to ...

Laurent: But I think what Don is saying, is his definition is much broader. And that's what I struggled with.

Don: Baba's definition is broader than that, because stored wisdom is simply the sanskaric ashes of your own incarnated experiences to help you in leading a more decent and natural life.

Laurent: I think Baba says it is actually *distilled* in the after-life experience. The wisdom is distilled there.

Female Participant: That would have stored *my movement toward the fruition of the whim.* All my stored wisdom will be my work in past lives, stored intuition, to bring me nearer to the whim, wouldn't it?

Don: Well, I think it's a glorious definition and a glorious aim. I just have a sneaky suspicion though that it isn't quite totally realistic in relation to the work [to be done, or] even Baba's definition of intuition, that's all.

Laurent: I think the key is ... Isn't there a difference in the caliber of a communication from the "drop-soul, Avatar, God," and the caliber of your own path experience? I would think there is some difference, some *qualitative* difference.

Don: Yes. Well done.

Keith: *That is exactly what I was going to say.* I mean, I can understand drop soul, Avatar, God, from Baba, is very pure, and very rare. The second one, the inherited one, it suddenly struck me, in our work, that it's associated with *confidence*. Because I've always been amazed at myself, when I've been able to do herbal formulas for the individual person. And I thought – Why, where did that come from? It came so easily, so quickly. – And so that bang, bang, bang. And it felt right. Now, I just wondered if that's what it was, inherited …

Don: All right. Let me carry you right down to one of our …

Keith: Let me just say one more thing, *I don't understand the third one.*

Don: The third one. Almost nobody does, so I'm not going to be able to clear that one up today, Keith. But certainly one does need to reflect on the role of sanskaras in the functioning of intuition. Let me put it broadly that way.

Keith: And how much work is there to do on sublimation?

Don: Well, uh …

Keith: Quite a lot.

Don: Sublimation is, as I've suggested, very much like selfless service. It is tremendously important, key and valuable. There is so much value to it, that one just has to search and see if there isn't something in one's environment which strikes one as so desperately important that one can say – I'm going to select that problem, and in some way I'm going to try to get closer to it. – Then you start trying to work on it, and then, oddly enough, little by little you begin to find that it naturally captures your own inner system of focused attention and sense of value. You just naturally begin to cotton more and more to it.

Baba says selfless service is like that. Helping other people has such a tremendous verity associated with it that, if you try, that verity is going to establish itself in you, and you find you do it for real. And sublimation, I'm convinced, is the same sort of process.

Laurent: Let me get us on to the *Three Bridges*, or else nobody will be happy with us.

❡ Don: Yup. We've got twelve minutes. That's four minutes per bridge. That's going to be some fast traveling.

Participant: Have you got time to talk about *Manonash*?

❡ Don: Manonash. Manonash, yes. I'm glad you brought that up. It's too important to risk losing. Because everybody thinks of it as the annihilation of mental processes, of the mind. After all, that's what it should be. And then, presumably, one goes on living only by the heart.

But let's listen to Baba himself and what he says about Manonash. This is taken from the biography, *Lord Meher*, which is quoting Baba here. I would like to go back to the original leaflet that I got directly from Adi Irani, to be absolutely sure it's correct, but this is what Bhau has written.

Laurent: They say it is in Purdom.

❡ Don: Yes, but I'd much rather go to Adi Irani, even than Purdom. I trust Adi Irani even more. Anyway, here we are. Here's Baba, and he's telling the people he is addressing that day, what goes on in Manonash, and what it is. "This means that when the mind, with its satellites …" Listen carefully to this, "… when the Mind with its satellites, desires, cravings, longings is completely consumed by the fire of Divine Love, then the infinite, indestructible, indivisible eternal self is manifested." But what is destroyed? He lists them here. These are the components of mind that are being destroyed: desires, cravings, longings. Doesn't that sound like the content of sanskaras that Baba describes to us again, and again, and again?

See Meher Baba's *Life Circular* No. 1, the February 6, 1952 message dictated by Baba about his Manonash work also found in *Lord Meher* Volume 10, pp 3759–3762.

Laurent: Sure.

⸿ Don: That's how Baba describes what they are. So it is not all of mind, but it is the sanskaric part of the storehouse in the mind that is destroyed. It is not mental processes, it's not your sense of equilibrium, your balance, reasoning and so on. That's not the "mind" that is being destroyed. Isn't it amazing? Baba puts it out so clearly, and yet we've tended to go way off on a sidetrack for a long time now.

Laurent: What about the second half of that one?

⸿ Don: Nope. It's a good one but we'll have to do that part another time. Now, so what … Nine minutes for three bridges?

Laurent: You *have to say* about the Three Bridges.

⸿ Don: All right. I've already told you the story about running around to see those people who knew Baba years ago, and finding all the interesting things they'd collected of various addresses given, that were never printed before [nor after], and this crucial, crucial statement that Baba made in one of them – Yes, I am the Avatar, and it is an important job in creation, but in the last analysis I am only a bridge to the Reality, which is God Himself. –

That is the first thing, and certainly the presence of the Avatar in the flesh is exactly what Baba says it is. He is describing himself. It is just that simple, and he uses the term "bridge." Then just a few days ago, I amazed myself by finding at this crucial moment, in a book devoted to the ancient *Jain* wisdom that this is a central term that they used and have used for thousands of years. This really floored me.

Jains are very, very ancient in India. And this concept of the bridge as being fundamental in the spiritual transit from earth to heaven, is embedded as a fundamental principal by the Jains … that where this concept originates was long before Baba.

For more about Jainism look for material about the Jain Spiritual Master, "Mahavir" who lived around 600 B.C.E. —Laurent

So that is [bridge] number one. Certainly Baba functioned as the bridge to God, because his every effort was exactly that.

Mani always used to say, "He's playing that person like a fish on a hook, and when he gets them on the hook, the real work starts." *It was all aimed at Baba getting the person attached to the need, the necessity, of getting onto the spiritual path to God, and he was the bridge. He was the fisherman. He was the line. He was even the hook. And boy, he could really play you.*

Sometimes you'd see Baba with a new person and you'd say – My gosh, he's buttering them up. – You'd almost have suspicions about what he was up to, you know. Sometimes I'd have trouble controlling myself, not to think thoughts I shouldn't be thinking. But at any rate, he did it. He would play absolutely everything that he could bring into it. He was a very clever man, very innovative, inventive. So he would get the fish on the hook, and then the real work would begin from there on. You can't get off the hook once you're hooked. So enough about the Avatar. You know that one.

Now for the second [bridge]. When Baba left [the physical body] this idea of the bridge was so firmly rooted in my mind that I said to myself – Well, Baba impressed upon me (when we were talking together about this business of meditation) that he provides for the time in the future when he will not be around. – He said to me, after I did all of those discourses on meditation, that because he wouldn't be around [physically] when eventually the Path of Love would narrow, that he had to provide [these discourses on meditation] for the future.

Now I saw, not just that one [example] – it was one of the most indelible ones – but example after example of how he knew and prepared for the future. He was responsible. And he knew what was going to happen. Then I said to myself – what's going to happen now? – For two or three years I didn't go to India, I just stayed away. Eventually I got a letter, a personal letter, from Eruch, saying – Don, you haven't visited us for a long time and you know, we're very close together, we're close friends with each other. We miss you. Why don't you come? – Something like that. It was simple, plaintive and human. And I kicked myself all over the lot, because there are any number of the Mandali that I love deeply and dearly. It's sincere relatedness. And I believe in relationship. So I said – This is a hell of a way for me to have treated these terribly, terribly close ones to me. –

Then I went [to India], and when I got there, just moseying around saying hello and seeing all of the Australians, and the French, and the Americans running around hither and yon, they all seemed to be saying, "Boy, it isn't like it was in Baba's day!" But then I went to a couple of meetings over at Meherazad, and I saw Eruch (above all) functioning in Mandali Hall. Eruch didn't sit in Baba's chair, but Eruch sure sat on his legs and gave forth. Then I saw how Mehera, and Mani, and the rest of [the Mandali] were functioning in relation to all these people flocking in. And I said – *Beloved God, it's obvious. Baba set them up as the second bridge.*

That was it. And it's working beautifully. So I just kicked myself for not having been intuitive, and figuring out ahead of time that maybe those close ones to Baba would be the next important bridge to get people over to God. They did a beautiful job, absolutely superb. Baba had imbued so much of Baba's love into them that it functioned marvelously.

Then, three or four years ago I began saying to myself – *Good heavens, even the Mandali are dying off thick and fast here. Soon they're going to be gone, too. Wow, there's the second bridge going, and we're not even a hundred years into the seven hundred years. What's going to happen in the other six hundred years? –*

Not long after that, almost as if it were a timed answer, I began to be aware of the fact that some extraordinary things, that I couldn't explain naturally, were beginning to happen in relation to *God Speaks*. And all of a sudden, a crazy episode occurred one morning at intuition time. Completely unexpected I said to myself – Should I take Baba seriously in his choice of the title for the book [*God Speaks*]? Did he mean that God was really speaking? – I asked myself that for the very first time. I said – Heavens, I wonder. I think maybe this is absolutely true. –

I began composing an article for *Neti Neti*. I don't know if you were there, Bruce, but I said, "This should be the lead article. Should we take Baba seriously?" Meanwhile, another improbable sequence of events. I had been going around saying, "We've got to start studying, working, with *God Speaks*." But I didn't say anything about the importance of the title. Then old Dick Duman gets a copy of the [Myrtle Beach *God Speaks* seminar] film and writes to me, – Don, did you realize that you said, "That when Ivy Duce sent the mock-up that she had done of the Dedication [in *God Speaks*]: 'To the Universe – the Illusion that sustains Reality' {Don makes an aside to the audience that this dedication always bugs him, and bothered him intellectually} – "that Baba spent hours going over this with Mani before she could get the right words…"

And Dick said, "That sounds a bit unusual." I wrote back immediately, and said, "Dick, I know it seemed to me like a long time that Mani expressed in that letter that I skimmed through, but I certainly didn't exaggerate it that much." Dick replied, "Well, I was trained as a lawyer, and I want to see a photocopy of the letter." Dear old Dick Duman. It was not exactly the time when it was convenient to get Dick his photocopy. I had stored all of these direct communications with the Mandali and Baba out at Debbie Sanchez's home, about thirty-forty miles away from where I was.

I thought – I'm not going to go over there, forty-fifty miles, and make a photocopy and then send it off. Much as I love Dick Duman, he can be impossible at times. – He sure could be.

I was kissing this whole matter off when, all of a sudden, I said to myself, – Don, come off of your high horse. If you sit and look honestly, you will remember that in two days' time there will be a group meeting at Debbie Sanchez's [home], and you've got to go over there. And Debbie is a sweet gal, and she will go to go get the file out. Also if you remember it correctly, you [already] put that letter on the top of the folder, because it had to do with an interesting problem.

As a matter of fact, a couple of days later we're there, and Debbie goes and gets it out and I take a look at it. But before going into the actual contents, I have to switch back to Myrtle Beach. Somebody there had gotten the movie out, and found that I actually had grossly exaggerated. I felt ashamed. It's not my nature to exaggerate.

There I was, all ashamed taking a look at this letter in Debbie's kitchen. Sure enough, *Mani says Baba spent quite some time before she could get, I think ... Could she have mentioned even ten-fifteen minutes, or something like that? It was a short time. It certainly wasn't hours on end.* I felt so badly about that, that I put it back in the envelope. Later, when I was driving home (with Claude Longuet) I thought to myself – Actually I remember that when I read that letter, I was busy. I was on a field trip. – I'd get copies of these long letters to Ivy Duce, copy to Don from Mani. There were very intensive, complex things that were being discussed, and I'd put them aside. I'd read just quickly over what seemed like the important material, and if it looked like it was drifting off, I'd put them in a file, even unread, and say to myself – Well, I'll read all of that later.

Now here we are, *forty years later*, and Stevens still hadn't even gotten to the end of that letter. But at least this time, I had read to the end of what [Mani] said [about the Dedication in *God Speaks*] – *It took me some time to get the exact wording.* – So then I go on. I say – Well, this time I'm going to do my duty. I'm going to read the remaining two, three paragraphs. – And as I did, I found that the next sentence, after taking some time even to get started, said, *"Now, Ivy, about your idea of auctioning off your baroque pearls that you bought in Saudi Arabia, before you do that, Baba wants to suggest that you might want to approach..."* so and so, and so and so, [several of the Baba people who liked jewels, and had a bit of money] "... and they might want to buy them, instead of putting them up for auction."

Forgive me, I've told this story three, or four times, but you've got to listen to it again. I've no use for baroque pearls, never liked them, and I thought these were amongst the most horrible I'd ever seen, so it had not been a popular item in my particular Ivy Duce inventory, after she bought them. Every two or three months she would say, "Don, I've got a wonderful idea. I'm going to auction off those pearls to make money from them..." for this and that project for Baba. And then something would always go wrong. Two or three months later, exactly the same thing. And two or three months later, another time, she'd be auctioning off her pearls for another wonderful Baba project. Finally, every time the word "baroque" or "pearl" came up, I turned off. I just literally turned off.

So what had I done with Mani's letter, getting so many Baba comments to Ivy Duce's baroque pearls? I got to the paragraph about the pearls, and auctioning them again... (Murshida, please don't listen to this) So here is Don ... I remember, at that point, I'd set it aside, and only two, three months before receiving Dick Duman's request for a photocopy of Mani's letter on the Dedication to *God Speaks*, when I'd been sending papers to Meheru, I had thought she ought to have the originals. But when I got to the point even then, of sending my original to Meheru, I put it aside again not fully read, and there we were.

Now, at long last I was reading it completely for the first time. You know what the rest of that sentence says? You should try so and so and so and so to raise the money, *"...because Baba wants you to know that in the future when people see, understand the enormous importance of the words in this book, they will realize that they come direct from God Himself."*

When you experience something like this, where you see how Baba has planted something forty years before, with such careful attention to detail, it touches something very deep inside you. In his own way, Baba gets all of these timing factors coordinated so that it comes out just at the critical time. So I telephoned *Neti Neti* and I said, "Hold the press, I'm going to write a second story. Let's keep the first story in, but tell the second story of what has happened, because this is really earth-shaking." So, I simply said to myself – Well, we've got the tradition of God blazing the *Ten Commandments* on Mt. Sinai. That is God, direct. Mohammed said that the words [of the *Koran*] were not his, that they came from God, and I think even many people who are not Muslims believe that he was an honest person, and he was telling the truth. Now, I said, here we have got this amazing third example of *God's direct words*. So, you see, I had had blazoned into me the importance of *God Speaks*. I'd done a lot of work on it. Then suddenly to take it as God's direct words. I said – This Baba is doing something now, and it's important. This has to be an important part of the structure of the *Third Bridge*. – Well, the Third Bridge is about to be put in position, and it's got to go into action promptly, and effectively. And a lot of these crazy ideas about – Well, *God Speaks* is too dense, it's just not for me – and so on. Some way or another we've got to break through it. That was the reason for the original *God Speaks* seminars … to see if a breath of Reality, of the importance of *God Speaks*, could be brought in here.

Then, when I was thinking about the third bridge, and starting up all this [series of seminars on Meher Baba's Word] two or three people said, "Well, Don, all of these other things that have been important in Baba's ministry aren't just going to disappear. Are you trying to imply that it is *God Speaks*, and only *God Speaks*, which is the third bridge?" And I said, "Good heavens, that probably is the implication that I've given so far."

Then the next morning at 3:30 AM comes this intuition, where, see this: something like a TGV [very fast train] in France with a nice dining car, rolling across a bridge, and a nice big buffet luncheon laid out there, and all sorts of people, and a nice big central hot dish labeled *God Speaks*. But there were other dishes around it. One of the other principle dishes is, "*contact with Baba Himself, intuitively*." But this, one should not look for too often. I just have to say that.

I know we mustn't expect that to be a constant dish, every day. I've had the dish, I'm convinced, three times since Baba dropped the body, and that's pretty far and few in between. Then there is another very large dish labeled, *"The Mandali and the close ones."* People are talking about how [the Mandali] are going to be reincarnating and coming back. And I believe that, too. I also believe that the beauty of the lives, and the biographies that a number of close ones to Baba have written, are an enormous resource. You know, the Muslims have sort of a three-tiered process of rating works in relation to Mohammed. And the top tier is the book from Mohammed himself, the Koran.

Then we've got things that are very carefully researched out: the close ones. Do you realize that Mohammed called them his *companions*? Does this ring a bell for you? This word is so important. And remember Eruch telling me, when I said, "Eruch, I don't know how you got through the New Life with all the hardships you put in." And Eruch says, *"Don, I've failed you. Because I have not given you the really important thing, that was companionship with the Avatar. That was Reality. And that was so wonderful."* So companionship is something there for real.

I also think that there are all sorts of ways that Baba has put the functioning of the provisional ego into activity. I've been absolutely amazed, as I told you, how he put a vow, of honesty to him, into action, and how that functioned in my own personal life. So we've got a variety of things that Baba has given. *They are not going to disappear*. They're certainly not. They're available. To me, what I seem to see in my funny little dream in the morning … as I saw the TGV going by on the Third Bridge – yes, a great big important dish, and the hot one on it is *God Speaks*, and other words given direct by Baba, as he clearly defined.

But that's not the totality of it. There are the marvelous lives of the Mandali, and *most importantly, our relation internally with Baba himself*. They're all terribly important parts of the buffet luncheon. So that is, you know, what I believe, has been provided. But we have got to appreciate what has been provided, and be terribly careful of our heritage. We must take the responsibility, a great big chunk of it, for preserving what he actually put there, and keep it from deteriorating as fast as Dharma usually decays in between Avataric incarnations. That is the challenge to us.

Ten minutes overtime. [Good work. Within budget] Yes, within budget.

Should we be silent for a moment?

DES Index

In Don's proof copy of Meher Baba's Word & His Three Bridges we found he had created a hand written index for himself, and perhaps for publication. We didn't know of its existence until 2021, and we are happy to finally share it here for the first time.

DES Index

This book was designed by Edmond Legum.

*The text face is Cycles, an elegant font of both calligraphic &
inscriptional character designed by Sumner Stone.
It is supplemented by Alisal, designed by Matthew Carter,
Amalthea, designed by Ernst Schneidler, &
Blado, a suberb italic designed by
Ludovico degli Arrighi
about 1526.*

The paper is made by Glatfelter.

❖

www.ingramcontent.com/pod-product-compliance
Lightning Source LLC
Chambersburg PA
CBHW051723040426
42447CB00008B/948